The Journey of Consciousness: A Warrior's Tale

An Eloheim and The Council Book

Veronica Torres

ISBN: 978-1-936969-15-9
Copyright 2011 Veronica Torres
eloheim.com
Published by Rontor Presents
Cover Design by Holly's Creative Design
hollyscreative.com
Mary T. George, Interior Formatting and Design
epubpub.com
Illustrations and Cover Art by Randy Sue Collins
thanknature.com

For Peter
Who taught me not to be afraid.

For Sasha
Who can fix anything.

and

For Jon
My "brother from another mother."

Acknowledgements

Over the years, I have read many, many books. I never understood why authors listed so many people in the acknowledgements. I always imagined writing to be such a solitary task.

Now that I am an author, I know the truth; writing doesn't happen in a vacuum.

I want to thank Sue Trainor for her calm presence and epic transcription skills; she is a true friend.

Mary Ricci cuts through the bullshit both as an editor and an observer of life; she is a trusted ally.

Leslie Hveem entered my life at the perfect moment. She helped me break through stagnate patterns and facilitates me offering the most current version of me to the world. Learn more by visiting: lesliehveem.com.

Elizabeth Erickson is an amazing cello teacher who also has the super hero power of discovering typos and other errors that no one else sees. Her website is: knightlizardmusic.com.

Randy Sue painted the cover of this book and drew the illustrations inside. I love her vision of the Warrior's words. It's awesome to have talented friends! You can learn about her work by visiting: thanknature.com.

Holly has designed the covers for all of my books. She is amazingly easy to work with. Learn more on her website: hollyscreative.com.

Mary "Genius" George more than lives up to her nickname. She formats our books, manages our technology, and is constantly learning new things to facilitate sharing The Council's teachings with the world. I am deeply grateful for her steady shoulder in this rapidly changing landscape. She can help you publish your book. Visit her website: epubpub.com.

Margy is the best "fake mommy" on the planet and I consider claiming her as such one of my wisest acts. I aspire to love the way she loves; it's unshakable. I'm often referred to as "fiery;" Margy's love is fuel on that fire.

Thank you all,

Veronica

November 2011

Contents

Introduction vii

Preface ix

One 1

Two 3

Three 7

Four 11

Five 15

Six 19

Seven 21

Eight 25

Nine 27

Ten 31

Eleven 35

Twelve 41

Thirteen 45

Fourteen 49

Fifteen 53

Sixteen 57

Seventeen 61

Eighteen 65

Nineteen 69

Twenty 73

Twenty-one 79

Twenty-two 83

Twenty-three 87

Twenty-four 91

Twenty-five 95

Twenty-six 97

Twenty-seven 101

Twenty-eight 105

Twenty-nine 109

Thirty 115

Thirty-one..**119**

Thirty-two **125**

Epilogue...**131**

Tools...**133**

    Clarity vs. certainty.. 133

    Feet under shoulders 137

    How ridiculous does it have it get? 139

    I don't know anything 141

    Lay it down and walk away.. 145

    Mad scientist.. 149

    Neutral observation 153

    "No" is a complete sentence / Say "no" first 157

    Point fingers... 159

    Preferences/Judgments 161

    Script holding/Script-holders... 163

    Strongest chakra 167

    Vulnerability vs. weakness 169

    What is true now?... 171

    What's in your lap? 173

    Where am I lying to myself? 175

    "Wow!", not "why?" 177

    You to you – U2U (comparing) 181

Terms **183**

    2012.. 183

    3D 183

    4 billion 183

    5D 183

    Abundance 184

    Aha 184

    Akashic Record.. 184

    Alternate expressions 185

    Amnesia.. 185

    Appreciation brings you into the moment 185

    Ascension... 185

    Audience or opinion.. 186

    Aura.. 186

    Baggage... 186

Being a question mark 186
Bliss 187
Boundaries 187
Boundaries with consequences 187
Brain 188
Bunnies and rainbows 188
But and because 189
Certainty 190
Chakra 190
Change... 191
Channel 191
Channeled message... 191
Checking things off your list... 191
Choose your reactions to your creations 192
Compassion 193
Complex vs. complicated.. 193
Conscious/Consciousness... 194
Consciousness-based operating system (CBOS)............... 194
Core Emotion (CE).. 194
Courage 194
Courageous enough.. 195
Creating your reality... 195
Creator, The 195
Creator/creatorship.. 196
Cultural pressures.. 196
Density 196
Digging a ditch... 196
DNA pressures 197
Don't bring your baggage to the moment......................... 197
Duality... 197
Earth 197
Ease 198
Ease not easy... 198
Easy 198
Eloheim 199
Emanating (the truth of you)... 199
Energetics 199
Ensoulment... 200

Fear..200
Fear-based 201
Fear-based operating system (FBOS)..........................201
Fear is a choice not a mandate....................................201
Fire hose 201
Free will..202
Free-will zone..202
Fulfillment 202
Gate latch 203
God 203
Going to see the king..203
Going with the flow 204
Grace..204
Growth 204
Guides..204
Habit/Habitual response 205
Hamster-wheel thinking...205
Healing..205
Heart–power chakra combination 205
High-vibrational..206
Hoarding...207
Homo spiritus 207
Insight..207
Jackets on the coat rack..207
Joy...208
Karma 208
Lack..208
Landing 208
Lateral pass...208
Layers of the onion 209
Light worker 209
Learning 209
Low-vibrational..209
Marble sculpture 210
Math problem 211
Mind..212
Mob mentality..212
Money flows, not grows..212

Mt. Everest.. 212
On the bus.. 213
Overachieving light worker.. 213
Peace.. 213
Personality... 214
Power 214
Proof.. 214
Protect what's mine... 215
Safety... 215
Sandpaper/Sandpaper people.. 215
Serenity.. 215
Service mentality.. 215
Shadow.. 217
Shake shoulders.. 217
Soul 218
Soulmate.. 218
Soul's perspective.. 219
Spirituality... 219
Spiritual discipline 219
Spiritual growth 219
Static 219
Suffering... 220
Survival Instinct 220
Thinking.. 221
Time.. 221
Tools.. 221
Transformation... 222
Triggers 222
Triggers are handholds 222
Unconscious... 223
Understanding is overrated.. 223
Unfolding... 223
Vibration 223
Victim/Victimhood 224
Woman by the campfire... 224
Your internal world creates your external journey 225
About the author **227**
What is channeling? **229**

vi

Who are Eloheim and The Council? **231**
Contact..**235**
Preview of other books..**237**

Introduction

The Warrior's story was originally channeled (narrated) between March 17, 2010 and January 5, 2011. You can learn more about this process in the appendix. Each chapter represents a separate session with the Warrior.

The Warrior has always referred to himself as "we." He never says, "I." It is rather unusual for a narrator to take this perspective and I did consider changing it for the book. However, I decided that it just felt right to leave it as it was originally given.

In the first seven chapters, the Warrior focuses on introductory material. From chapter eight on, the focus changes to the Warrior's "fairy tale for grown-ups." You will visit castles, kings, battles, and beasties, all of which will illuminate and instruct your spiritual journey.

The Warrior speaks quite a bit about spiritual tools. He is referring to the tools that have been presented during our nine years of channeling sessions. I have included 17 of these tools in this book. It may be helpful to review them before beginning.

Additionally, I have included definitions of 126 terms and concepts that have come from our channeling sessions. They can be found following the tools.

When the Warrior first introduced himself, I was intimidated by his big energy and powerful message. As he continued to offer his teachings and as he evolved his heart, I developed a bit of a crush on him.

He is a unique figure not often found in these times. I am so very grateful for his presence in my life.

Preface

This entire story is to help you know who you are.

We will hold the space for you to safely explore that which you have been hiding from yourself, but we cannot force you to do so. You have a place within you that looks dark, that's black, perhaps. Hold that space within you, allow yourself to know this space and know the truth of you and to become aware of the lies you've told. Know the hiding you've done and allow yourself to bring this truth to your knowingness.

We just want to open the door to that truth, to help you become aware of the lies, to open the door to the part of you that you have been unwilling to know. When this space is cleared, it gives you the opportunity to create your life in a brand-new way. A brand-new way. We are here to hold the space. Do you understand? We are not here to do it for you. We are here to reach inside of you, open it up, let you see what's there, and then support you in letting it heal. Letting it transform. Our role is that we are not afraid of any of it. Hear us now. *You cannot show us anything that creates fear within us.* If it creates fear within you, we invite you to allow our energy to permeate the space and to stand beside you without fear. We don't even experience courage. We experience the absence of the possibility of fear. And we hold you in that truth. We hold you in the truth that says, "There is no fear here." What there is is the willingness to tell yourself the truth.

We are able to stand in non-judgment, non-duality, and hold the truth of you regardless of the acts you have committed. Regardless of the thoughts you have had. Regardless of the urges of the body. We are able to stand in the place that holds who you truly are aside from the judgments and dualities that your physical life have lumped onto the truth of you. As you shed those things, you give yourself the opportunity to stand the way we stand. We invite you to join us in this stance.

They call us the Warrior primarily because we are willing to face anything. Not for love of country or any of the things that previously you may have experienced warrior energy around, but for the revelation of truth; the revelation of the completeness of you experiencing the human form and the revelation of you knowing the completeness of you while in the body. You're ready for it. We stand next to you as you reach out and reclaim yourself from the way it has had to be in order to experience humanity up until this point. There is a door now open that has not been open to you before, and you do not walk through it alone. We invite you to acknowledge your willingness and acknowledge your readiness because those are two far, far different things. Anyone can be willing but it requires someone with courage to be ready. You will not walk alone. You will have tools.

You are not alone. We stand next to you knowing the truth, knowing the complete story, and we are neither shocked nor dismayed. You have never been in the presence of a being that can hold the stance of non-judgment the way we can, for that is the strength we bring.

One

We sit by a campfire as we speak to you. It's night. At the dawn the trumpets will blare. The horses are there, waiting to be saddled. Over to the side we have the young boys sharpening and tending and mending things. We sit here in a circle with the others. We have many, many, many battles and campaigns under our belts. Many little trophies and remembrances of grizzled experiences, and there are scars. You'd be quite terrified, we imagine. You don't see many like us in the physical incarnation you're currently experiencing, but you have it in your genetic memory. You know. As we sit here in front of this fire, and we look and we see the stars above and the trees surrounding us, the truth of who we are is undeniable. Why? Because the only moment that we exist in is the moment of readiness, the moment of "prepared for," and that's the invitation we extend to you.

Join us in the moment of readiness, the moment of "prepared for." Note that "prepared for" is not followed by a bunch of bullshit. Prepared for. Period. Ready. Period. We know not what we'll face on the morrow. We know not what we will face, and neither do you. You can only be ready, prepared for, and that is only understandable, experience-able, where? The moment. So welcome to our camp. We are prepared. We can sit still like this, prepared, for a very, very, very long time, until it is appropriate to act.

When you want our energy, come to our fire. Make your presence known so you don't get stuck with something sharp. It could happen. There are lots of sharp things about. Speak up, say who you are and what it is you wish to learn at the fire, what it is you wish to experience, what it is you wish to feel. All you need to say is, "I am here and I am willing to sit in a new energetic." That's all. But it's a lot.

Two

Every field of battle we have walked onto has required rooting out the enemy. We climb trees and we look in holes and we go under waters, and we do what we have to do to find those that hide from us. And they hide. They all hide. There's always someone hiding, just waiting to shoot us in the back or get behind our lines or do other kinds of mischief. Sometimes they're cowards. Sometimes they're brave. It doesn't matter. They're looking for information and for survival. It's OK. We still find them. You don't get to do this for as long as we have without knowing the places where they hide.

So we say the same thing to you. You don't get where you're going unless you know the places where you hide your shit within you, because that's where your field of battle is. Is it in that stiff neck of yours? Is it in that bum knee? How about that low back? What do you have hiding in there? They're favorite hiding spaces; the enemy knows them. You have made your shadow your enemy; therefore, it hides from you with the sneakiness and guile of an enemy. You don't even know where it is. Some of you have so little experience on the field of battle that you don't even know where to begin looking for these things that are hiding from you. In that case, we encourage you to get a little more experience, because one of the only places you learn this fight is in the fight itself. Take yourself into it and explore: where are you hiding? If you feel a pain, ask yourself, "What am I hiding there?"

At a minimum, you're hiding shame about the pain, embarrassment, difficulty, dismay. When you have a pain and you accept it, "I created that pain. I take 100 percent responsibility for that pain presenting itself in my body," that's how you root it out. That's how you climb the trees and shake the enemy out like acorns. That's how it's done. Every time you walk onto the field of battle you have to "man up." You have to be brave, courageous, insane sometimes, it doesn't matter. The bottom line is you have to stand in your power, even if shit runs down your leg as you do it, because unless you stand there in your power you're running away. There are only two options: You stand or you run.

You don't have to know what to do. You just have to stand in willingness to do it when clarity arises. You have to take responsibility for finding yourself on that field in the first place and take responsibility for the encounters you have therein. Honor. That's another word for it. Honor. You're being honorable. You're only accountable to yourself. You don't even have a bastard king to cut off your head if he doesn't like what you've done. Trust us, those are not fun.

You're responsible for your tools and the maintenance of them. You are responsible for sharpening and cleaning and mending and carrying at the ready the tools that support you on the field. You say, "Oh, I didn't think about that." Well, that's consciousness. Bring to the front of you your readiness, your courage, and your assets. Hold them in front of you. Have them ready. Don't leave them behind when it's time. When you go exploring the places within you that you've hidden from—the pains, the aches, the anxieties, the fears, the terrors—don't start on that journey unless you have given yourself the opportunity to arm yourself. And by this we mean you feel a pain and you think, "Oh, I'm going to go look at that pain. What do I want to take with me?" Ask yourself, "What do I want to take with me on that journey to that battlefield? Well, I want to take with me being in the moment, being conscious."

Get yourself ready. Arm yourself with four or five of these tools that you know you like, that work well for you. Remind yourself, "What tools might I need?" Don't start using them, just pretend you're us and lay them out in front of you: your knife, your bow, your axe, your hatchet, your sword, lay them out. Are we using them? No. We're laying them out and making sure they're ready. This you can do too. Lay them out and make sure they're ready, all right? And then, once you've refreshed yourself about them, then and only then, you go into the battle. Go to the pain and talk to the pain and see what it has to teach you. But let yourself be ready with your tools first. Do you understand?

Sometimes what happens is you go exploring and you forget to have your tools at the ready, you show up with your eating knife and nothing else. We don't recommend taking on the enemy with your eating knife, at least not when you could have brought all the other stuff with you, had you prepared. When you explore yourself, prepare. That doesn't mean you're creating from a negative place. It means you're preparing for the encounter in a conscious way. It's not, "Oh, what will I need?" It's, "Damn right, I'm going to need some things. I'm going to take everything I can and I'm going to take them from a place of refreshed memory." Just like we sit by the fire and sharpen our tools, you sharpen your remembrance, sharpen your awareness of the tools you have.

This is very important. We would not send you into a fight unarmed, especially when you have the choice of weaponry right there all the time. It's a beautiful array. The armory is just waiting. You have permission to walk in and take whatever you wish. Yet, most of the time, we see you walk into battle with only your meat knife. Be kinder to yourself than that.

Three

The full moon is your friend sometimes. It's your foe at other times. We see the full moon and we say occasionally it lights your way and occasionally it makes you prey. It's hard. It's hard to know what to do under the full moon at times. If you're moving, it can help you. If you're waiting, it can hinder you. When you look at the moon, know it's telling you something. We ask, "Tell us moon, what is it that you have to say tonight?" And it says that it is here to light the path.

You do not want to hide. You do not want anything to hide from you. You are rooting out and seeking out things, so the moon is on your side tonight. It helps you. It helps you as you walk through the forest of the truth of you and as you look for things that are hiding behind trees and in bushes. As you look, look for the things within that shame you, that embarrass you, that confuse you, that you fear. The places within you where you say, "Oh, please, let no one ever find this."

The moon shines its light on everyone equally. We point this out to you so that you know that as you experience illumination, everyone has an equal chance. It's not like there's scarcity when it comes to illumination. There is no lack when it comes to illumination. All that's required is that you turn your eyes toward the truth. Allow the illumination, the illumination of your soul's insight to light up the dark places just like the moon shines on you. When the dark places are illuminated, look and see what you find. Do not hide and turn from it. Do not say, "Oh, this is something I should be ashamed of, this is something that I cannot face, this is unbearable." At a minimum, say yes to the unbearability of it all. "This is an unbearable place within me and I will say yes to the fact that I'm admitting it's unbearable." Instead of just sneaking around with your eyes covered, as though somehow the moon will not shine on someone whose eyes are covered, the rest of you is still bathed in moonlight even if you bind your eyes. This is a good analogy for the idea that you are surrounded by illumination even if you refuse to look at it. The truth of you is here. It only needs you to look at it and acknowledge it. You're hiding from the authentic experience of illumination. Regardless of your participation, it's occurring. Just like the moonlight. You try to hide from it and it's as silly as the ostrich proverbially sticking its head in the sand. There's still lots of the ostrich you can see and there's still lots of you being bathed in the truth of your shame. Even if you pretend you can't see it, it's still there. All that's required is you to say, "Yes, it's there." You can even say, "Yes, I'm still ashamed of it." But you must shift into "Yes, I see it's there" in order to return to the wholeness of you. You cannot go where we're going unless you take the wholeness of you.

We walk in the forest with you. We walk on the path you are creating. We are widening the path by giving you this information. But we do not carry you. We will not carry you. We will walk beside you. We will even give you an arm. We will even carry your things for you. But we will not pick you up off of your two feet and hoist you along the path. That, we will not do for you. For you have free will. And it is inappropriate for that to be done. Therefore, it is not going to happen. However, everything up and to that point that we can do for you, with you, and in collaboration, we will do. We will walk on that path through the forest creating a new way. Tirelessly. Carrying tools you've never even seen before. Tirelessly. But we will not force you to walk with us and we will absolutely not carry you. This is our covenant with you. That is our boundary. That's what a healthy boundary looks like.

The moon shines down on you and offers you its truth. What is the truth of the moon tonight? It shines its illumination on you just as your soul's insight and the truth of you is constantly illuminated within you. The only requirement is that you take away your hand from your eyes, that you open your eyes and you say, "I see the truth of me. I see the truth of me!" This is you standing on the field of battle. Afraid or not. But showing up and standing in the truth of you. Not projecting what's going to happen next. Not wondering how you've been before. Simply, amazingly, and authentically standing in the truth of you. Standing in the truth of you in the moment and then walking it forward through your energetic emanation, through your physical deeds, through your thoughts, and through your emotions.

One day, we will feel this in you. You are still at the point where it's a question mark, and we understand and there is no shame in that. But one day very soon, we will feel this in you and you will feel it in yourself. We stand beside you for as long as it takes, for that is our role. When you go out and you see the moon, remember our words. The moon shines on you and gives you an opportunity to experience the illumination of the truth of you. Let it. Let it shine on you and let the truth of you be illuminated. Just like the beauty of the moon shining, you will be a beacon of the truth. The moon doesn't have to know where its truth lands and you will not need to know where the truth of you lands, either. You simply need to stand with your eyes open, with your willingness to participate in the integrity of you at the forefront.

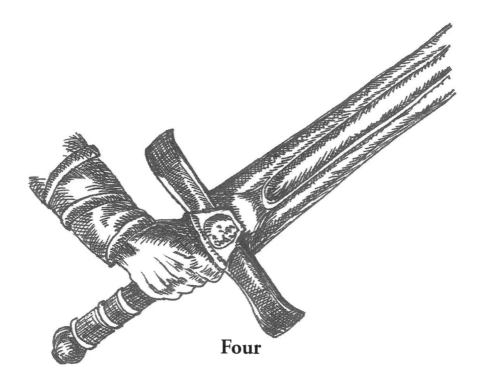

Four

Your journey is not just illuminated by the moon. It's illuminated by those that you walk with. It's illuminated by your soul. It's illuminated by your experience of the moment, and it's deepened as you allow yourself to deeply be in the moment.

One of the interesting things about the field of battle is that you can't think about anything else. You can't be on the field of battle and wonder what's going on with your cows. It doesn't work that way. That's a sure way to get yourself dead. That singular focus is actually addictive, and some people go looking for that singular focus and feel that the fight is the only place to get it. You have to be cautious about the idea that anything like that is true, for it is not that you must fight to be focused, but it is true that focus allows you to attend to what you're doing—whether it be fighting or milking cows—in a more profound and deep way. We invite you to allow focus to give you that edge. Not the edge over anyone, but the edge of overcoming your cultural conditioning, overcoming your habitual responses, and allowing yourself to be fully present and fully experiencing the truth of you.

The focus that's required is not coming from an external source. Again, *your* battlefield is within. Yours is within. You don't have someone coming at you on horseback with a sword to get you to pay attention. But you have within you someone coming at you with a sword. Someone who triggers you, someone who brings attention to something you're embarrassed by, someone who startles you into insecurity, someone who leaves their dishes in the sink when you don't like them to. Whatever it happens to be, all of those things will give you an opportunity to experience the focus that we find when we walk onto the battlefield. Your battlefield is you looking for the truth of you, cutting away that which hides it, cutting away that which pretends to be the truth of you, and allowing yourself to deeply, authentically, experience your truth. Bring this focus to your journey and you will find yourself victorious, and the victory is that you have deeply known yourself.

You have the opportunity to bring the focus of the master, the master at arms, to bring that kind of focus into this journey that you're on in this incarnation. Allow yourself to feel the strength in you. When you lift your sword and you feel the strength in your arm, when you ride your horse and you feel its power beneath you, when you scream your battle cry and you feel it in your loins—yes, those things are obvious strengths. For you, it is more the opportunity to face your triggers and have a "yes" at the ready. It is the sword in your strong hand. "Yes, I will say yes to you. And by saying yes to you, I vanquish you because you cannot stand in front of me. Because you are not a barrier to me, you are simply a pathway. When I say yes to you, you become the pathway. If I say no to you, you stand as a great foe." You can knock down those in your way with the "yes" to the fact of it, because your battlefield is so different than the one we like to describe.

Even in ours, saying yes to the fact someone is coming at us is much, much more appropriate than saying no. "No" is not going to stop the sword from swinging. "No" is not going to stop a trigger from approaching you. "Come to me, my enemy. Come close to me so that I may show myself who I am by interacting with you. I will know myself because I will have faced you." You will know yourself because you will have faced your triggers, and you will have faced them with the strong sword in your strong arm and your sword says yes, as it rings, as it interacts with the trigger. It screams, "Yes, I will be courageous." Again, courage is feeling the fear and doing it anyway. "I will be courageous in my yes and I will face my foe." In your case, your foe is a trigger, a habit, a fear, an anxiety, a past-life influence, a physical ailment, whatever it happens to be. It's not that it's easier than having someone swing a sword at you, but we will say it tends to be less bloody. And after a while, swords do get heavy, even for us.

Face your foes with courage, with fortitude, and your sword screams: "Yes! Come to me. Come closer to me that I may interact with you, engage with you and transform you into something that tells me who I am, that shows me the truth of me and that reveals my emanation to all who encounter me, including myself." Yes. Just hold your sword of yes. The truth of you is on the end of that word. The truth of you is revealed at the end of that syllable, that last bit of the S, just at the end, the truth of you is illuminated. "No" is more and more and more shields in front of you. "Yes" breaks you free. What if you fear that you won't like what you see? Well, at least you'll know what's there. Right now, it's all hidden, and we're not so proud of hidden. We're not so enamored of hidden. There is something about standing there in the skin that God gave you and saying, "Well, I may not be done with me, but I'm certainly not going to hide the truth of me any longer." Yes. We will see you stand like that. We know it's true.

Five

Standing at the edge of the battlefield on the eve of battle you may feel fear. What we mean by this is very important for us to illuminate to you. What we mean is that it is not that you are constantly ready. It's not that you are constantly courageous. It's not that everyone is ready and happy to be there. No. They're pissing and shitting and sweating themselves, but they do it anyway. They have many reasons to stand at the edge of the battle-field, but really, we want to focus on the way you stand at your battlefield, you stand in the moment and tell the truth about it. Tell the truth about the moment and experience yourself there. This is the opportunity of self-revelation. The opportunity to know yourself, to know who you are.

That is really the point of all of this, to know yourself. We call it a battle and we come off with the warrior energy and we talk about all these things because we want you to see that it is not something that you just lightly wade into like a river or the ocean. You're not going for a bit of a splash. You're going into serious confrontation with your shit and you're doing it because you know that to remove yourself from suffering and to enter into serenity requires transformation, and to experience transformation requires courage to face what is actually present.

We want you to be in *actualization* about what is occurring. Some will stand at the edge of the battlefield and want to deny the truth of the enemy over that next rise. They'll actually pretend the enemy is not there and that somehow they're off for some sort of exercise. We look at those and we think, "We'll be carrying you away." Do we say that in a way that's disrespectful? Of course not. We say it in a way that's truthful. If you're in denial of what is true, chances are the truth is going to catch up with you. When you're in battle, that truth will often slay you. Your denials have been slaying you. How have they slayed you? They have taken you out of serenity and bliss—even happiness—and left you in suffering, fear and anguish, that you cover up with drugs, sex, and TV. But the truth is, you know that there is more to be had in this life and you wonder how to have it. We don't just mean material possessions, but of course, that's part of it all.

What we mean is there's more to have that is experientially authentic, and to have that experience authentically you have to show up to the truth and experience the truth. The truth is what's really going on—whether it's a thought of some shadow that you're embarrassed or ashamed of, or it's a thought of some love that you are pleased with, or something in between—they are all the truth and we ask you: Are you ready to live in the truth? That's the question we have for you. Are you ready to stand at the battlefield in truth? Because if you don't, guess what? You get carried off. It doesn't just mean you get slayed. What it means is you don't live. You don't live if you don't live where the truth lies, and the truth is in this moment. If you're ignoring the truth of the moment, then what are you here for? Be in the moment with the truth of the moment and then experience and transform what you find. This is what we have to say to you. When you ask how, we say, "Well, we're here telling you as best we can different nuances of it, but the bottom line is: You show up." You show up and you stay where the moment is. Stay where the moment is, experiencing the truth of what you see and know, and ask for it to transform into something that is more constructive, more high-vibrational, and that moves away from fear.

Now, when it's said that way it sounds sort of easy and we understand that it's very challenging, but we also understand that you are a courageous warrior of this type. You wouldn't read this if you weren't, so it is just another battlefield that you're approaching. You choose how you enter this battlefield. You choose which tools you carry. You choose it all! It's all your choice. Own that it's your choice. The truth of it is you. Be that way. This is what we offer you.

When we stand next to you, even if you are shitting yourself, we will stand next to you proudly, if you stand there with the truth of you. Even what you consider your most embarrassing truths are far more powerful to us than candy-coated bullshit — or even less interesting, forays into the past or the future—when the moment is juicy and ready for you. You would pass up a beautiful meal to remember a snack or to hope that you would be fed again? Hah! We suggest you don't pass up the juicy meal. No warrior ever passes up the juicy meal. The moment is radically powerful. Ridiculously amazing. It's the only real thing here. We will continue to walk beside you and help you to remember. Until one day, you meet us and you stand beside us and you look to us and say, "Hah, there you are." We feel that day. We feel this truth. You have yet to feel it, but you will. So we stand in that truth already, and you will join us completely and on that day, a fine day will be had.

Six

We see you as we walk along here, we see you on this path in the forest, and the pathway is not well marked. You very well could be the first human that ever walked it. The deer and the rabbits and various other woodland creatures—otherwise known as lunch—amble along and hop and do whatever they do, but the opportunity for humans to tread this ground has been very limited. That's specifically why we're here. You want new vistas, you want new lands, you want new experiences, you want to experience the truth of you emanating in a new environment, you want to be you in a new way, or else you wouldn't be here. You wouldn't be experiencing this place and you wouldn't be walking on this path and you certainly wouldn't be with us.

So as you walk along this path, we see you—you are not yet very graceful. Branches slap you in the face and you're always scratching at your legs. God, you'd think that all the bugs on the planet have attached themselves to you. You oftentimes drop things and you never can quite walk without making an awful lot of noise. You are awkward, but it is the awkwardness of the newborn. Does anyone criticize the brand-new foal for not being able to walk when it has just hit the ground? Of course not. Of course not. That would be the most ridiculous thing you could do. For there is a fine animal ready to be your compatriot. It's just been born. It's a brand-new life. Think of the adventures you'll have together. To criticize or critique it for being wobbly is just…the idea of it is silly. We do not criticize or critique you. We simply acknowledge that you're a bit wobbly when it comes to this new path. It's all right.

However, at some point, you're going to need to get your shit together or else those previously mentioned woodland creatures will never stick around long enough for us to have lunch. Meaning you are not going to feel fed by your world unless you get to a point where you feel balanced in it. You are not going to feel nourished by your experience unless you're bringing yourself into a centered position in it. What we want for you is to recognize that it's OK to have wobbly legs and that this is an opportunity for you to bring balance to the new, wobbly legs that you have. It's an opportunity for you to continue to bring it all back to this moment. To continue, to continue, to continue, to take it back to what is true now, back to your integrity expressed, and back to what is real, the truth of you.

So, yes, you're a wobbly colt, but you're cute and someone will feed you for now. As you start to move more gracefully on this new path, you will start to experience more because you won't be scaring off all the woodland creatures. The truth is that you will start to experience more of your world because you're more present in it. You're more aware in it and you're more real in it. You live where the truth is. You understand? Just like as we walk along the path, we see much, much more than you do, because you're just so busy not getting smacked in the face by branches and things. Once you start to work with the environment in a new way it allows you to experience more of it. You understand us?

We very much enjoy the opportunity to interact with you this way and to spread our wisdom, because it is wisdom, after all, we're not afraid to acknowledge that it's wisdom. We're not ashamed or embarrassed to admit that we have wisdom. Are you? Sometimes you are.

We hope you have noticed that we have left the campfire and we are moving now. This is not simply to give you something else to picture. You are on the move and you are in good company.

Seven

It's very interesting how you have this money thing and you have value, value. It's very interesting to us because value to us is very, very frequently non-currency-based. We don't live in currency-based communities. Sure, there's currency and there are coins, but most often in the time we live in: "I'll do this for you and you will give me a horse. I'll take care of this little bit over here and you'll give me a bed for the night." We live more in a barter environment, and the beauty of barter is that the value is not generalized. With money, you generalize the value. "I will work doing whatever and you will give me x number of dollars and then those x number of dollars will be trotted off and done whatever with." The beauty of barter is that you don't generalize the value. However, you're not in a barter community, not primarily, at least. So you have the option to generalize the value of your work, if you care to. We advise you to discontinue generalizing your value.

Now, what's most important here is that your value is not based in how much you are paid for something, your value is based on how you perceive yourself within the transaction. The income or the goods bartered are simply a reflection of how you perceive yourself within the transaction. How do you perceive yourself in the transaction? Do you perceive yourself as a $10 person? Do you perceive yourself as $100 person? What does that mean? Do you see yourself as exchanging the truth of you and then receiving something of value in that moment? Your value can never be monetized, even if you're paid by the hour. It is not: "I go to work and get a certain amount of money." It's: "I go to work to grow and wow, I get paid." It's a radical shift of perspective about money; taking it out of the generalization position that it currently occupies and putting it in a consciousness position which allows other ways for money to come to you, because what you're saying is: "I don't trade myself for money. I show up as the completeness of me and I experience an abundant universe."

When we go out, most of the time it works something like this: Some royal something or other sends his representatives out to ring us up, as you would say, you can imagine what that's like. You can see them from a mile away, they make a lot of noise, and they smell sweet, which doesn't fit into any sort of environment we live in. They trot up and try to act like we're important, as if their behavior tells us who we are. This makes us laugh. We laugh at them and they don't understand why, and that makes us laugh even more. Then they'll say something to the effect of, "Lord such-and-so begs that you come and do blah blah," which usually involves sharp, pointy things, and we say, "Yeah, whatever." Then they start in with the: "and because you're so valuable we're going to give you x, y, z for doing it." Don't ever fall for that.

Don't ever fall for that part, do you hear us? Don't fall for that part. When you fall for that, then you are no longer your own man. You are his man. And you do not want to be his man. When you fall for the idea that he's telling you your value by giving you something for your efforts, you will not be able to stand with pride in yourself. So he'll say, "blah, blah, blah," and you'll say, "whatever," and you'll think, "Well, does it serve me?" Careful—not: "Does it serve him?" But "Does it serve me to participate in this escapade?" Most of the time, it's fun. We know you probably wouldn't find it fun, but that's OK. We would certainly never sit in front of a computer for six hours a day either. We have different job skills. So, sometimes, we just look around at each other and say, "What do you think, boys? Shall we go off with such-and-such?" and so forth. Typically, we say, "Yes." We have to make sure he doesn't smell like that for the rest of the journey, though, so we throw him in the manure and roll him around a few times. Who wants to travel with someone who smells like that? They don't particularly like that part, but by then, they think they have made us feel valuable. They think that we are part of their story now. Don't ever let them. Don't ever believe that they are telling you who you are. Don't ever believe that the way they tell you who you are has to mean who you are. And of course, by "they" we mean your boss, your employer, your clients even. They don't tell you who you are. Not with their money. Not with their smiles.

When someone comes up to you and says, "I'll give you $100 if you do x, y, z for me," that's not them telling you you're worth $100. That's you deciding if emanating your truth in their environment will be something valuable to you as a spiritual aspirant. That they give you $100 is just proof you live in an abundant universe. Do you understand this? Good. We wouldn't want to have to roll you in the manure, after all.

So, when they come to you and they offer you trinkets and gold and money or whatever—they're always trying to give us new clothes as though there's something wrong with the current ones we have. They think we smell. We know we don't—when they come to you, don't make the error in energetics of believing that they're telling you your worth. When they come to you and they offer you whatever they offer you to run off and use your pointy objects on something, ask yourself, "Can I be the truth of me in that environment? Does it please me; does it please me to be in that environment? Does it intrigue me? Does it fascinate me? Does it seem to give me an opportunity for growth?" The reward for you going out and being your complete self can be more abundance than you initially imagined if you actually take your complete self into that space. When you don't believe their value of you, then you tap into the possibility of the abundance of your universe showing up in the transaction.

Don't let them set your value. You know the truth of you. Emanate it and experience it in all situations to facilitate connection with the abundant universe you live in. You are not a dollar sign.

Eight

Now, we've come to a clearing. As we look out into this clearing, we remember something. We don't always like to recount some of these things. It's not easy to talk about those times when you do combat, when you fight yourself. Because that's what the enemy is, after all, is an expression of you, especially as you fight. As you face the enemy, as you face the foe, as you face the other combatant, as you feel your comrades stand next to you, they're all you. They're all you showing you, you. They're all you experiencing you. It's all you. It's all you. That's what makes the battle so painful.

That's what makes it so challenging. There's no one else to blame. There is no one else to look at. There's no one else to expect to have an answer. There is no one else to whom you can just say, "You, damn it, it was you all along." There is no one else. There's no one else. To get there you have to stop pointing fingers, because when you stop pointing fingers you stop making there be another. See, you are in training to know you're all one by not pointing fingers anymore. Pointing fingers keeps you in duality. Pointing fingers keeps you separate. And none of that is true, of course.

So, when we sit here at the edge of this clearing, we remember the screams. There are also the war cries, the yells of triumph, and the shouts of intense exhilaration. We don't remember those so much. What we remember are the screams. The screams. The horses, they scream. The people, they scream. Grown men scream for their mothers, their sweethearts, and their wives and children. You have screamed. You scream every day. "Why?" "Why is it so hard?" "Why am I still triggered by this?" "Why is it so confusing?" "Why can't I just know what to do?" "Why am I here?" "Why did I come here?" "Why? Why? Why?" You scream and scream again. You scream the scream of victimhood. On the battlefield, when you put your sword through another man and he screams, he's not screaming in triumph. He's not screaming in power. He screams mostly, not always but mostly, because he feels he's the victim of your blade. You scream because you feel you are a victim of someone else's blade. The screams, well, they're coming to an end now.

Just like now we look at this clearing and there are some butterflies, there's a rabbit or two—dinner—there's a deer, trees, birds. The screams are all hidden by the grass that's knee-high now. It's covered all the blood, all the pain. It's covered. And you, in your own way, are transforming your screams into a beautiful field, a place of growth, a place of blooming, a place of unfolding. That's what you're doing. Your journey and our journey have been very similar. You walk in the same footsteps that we walk. It looks a bit different, but your screams are loud. The nice thing is you have the ability to transform your relationship to your screams. You have the opportunity to open up to being in this blooming field of abundant potential. We meet you on the edge of this field and we ask, "Shall we go into the past and remember or shall we be in the moment and explore?"

Nine

Here we are at the meadow. As we sit here and look out at this field, we remember the last time we were here there was a battle. We want to tell you what's like at the end of a battle. We all stand around breathing hard and wondering just exactly how many of our parts are still attached, we look around. You know what there is to be seen. Bodies. The horses. The wagons, whatever else is around. There's always something else around. The weapons. The blood. Let's be honest. You still hear the cries. Maybe not the screams, but the cries, the whimpers. That last exhale as someone ends their incarnation. Most of this is difficult to hear just in this moment we are describing. It's difficult to hear, because all you can hear is the pounding of your heart and the breath coming in and out in such a ragged way. Your adrenaline is coursing through your body at such a rate that you feel hyper-aware but your body processes are so loud that they are taking up all your ability to perceive things.

So it's a sense of inhale, exhale, inhale, exhale, this deep breathing. It's the deep breathing. As you breathe this deeply, you start to become more aware of the smells and the sounds; you start to become more aware of your surroundings. You are still looking for danger, you're still looking for a foe, and you're still looking for what's coming at you. Slowly but surely you recognize there is no more to look for. There is no more to deal with. And—boom—everything is different from that point on. Because for all the time before, it was about the fighting, and now, it's about the aftermath. You have been doing a similar thing. You've been fighting and fighting and fighting within you. You've been fighting your habits. You've been

Veronica Torres

fighting victimhood. You've been fighting what it's like to be Homo sapiens. Now just as radically as the end of our battle, you have this change. It's that drastic. You change into something else. All of your attention changes.

Moving out of victimhood, moving into, oh, sort of taking responsibility and moving into not pointing fingers is such a radical change. It's such a big shift. It is similar in degree to the change we have described. You're asking yourself to use a new set of skills. Previous to this, your skills have been fighting and fighting and resisting, ducking, running, dodging, attacking, and now your skills are opening and allowing and seeing from a new perspective. It's a whole completely different paradigm you're entering. Instead of resisting, you're moving. You're moving *through* your creation rather than resisting it. You are dancing with your creation rather than fighting it. You're saying yes to your creation rather than trying to find a way to blame it on somebody else. You are not able to hide from the truth of your creation anymore, and that's really the key point of this whole thing. You can't hide from the truth of your creation anymore.

Whatever the truth of your creation is, we advise you to say yes to it, to open to it, to experience it deeply, to embrace it, because the truth of your creation is the doorway into the big picture of Homo spiritus living. We got you into the moment and now you need to say yes to the moment and ask, "Where am I lying to myself?" and "What is true now?" It's a whole different level now as you move into the truth of you being expressed without looking for someone else to take the blame. Without looking for someone else to be the fall guy. Without looking for somebody else to be the one that did it. There's no one else to take the blame for how you interact with your creation. There's only you choosing the "wow" or you choosing the "why?" That's your choice. "Am I going to choose wow or why?" Wow or why.

Now you say, "OK, I have this creation and I say 'wow, it's pretty fascinating' and I want to know why it's here." And we would ask you not to do that. Why? Because you want to shift your energy out of: "I have to think about it and understand it," into: "I'm experiencing it and allowing more." Allowing more. That's the whole point of this. You get more when you allow. When you wonder and think and have to have it explained, you get less. We have a strong suspicion you want the more. If you want the more, you go to "wow" and if you want it to stay the way it's been, then you can stay in "why" all you want. "Why" is limitation. "Wow" is expansion.

When you go in and allow more wow, well, then you start the process of living from your soul's perspective, seeing things the way your soul sees them. Your soul sees all as fascinating, all as interesting, all as educational, and all as helpful. It's exactly the beautiful creation, the detailed creation that you have presented yourself. All of it is ready for you to experience more of. You have to decide if you're going to be in the mode to experience more of it or to go and think about it. Part of that comes down to you having judgment about it, too.

Observe it neutrally. Believe it's going to teach you something. Go into wow. Same thing, just a different level of it. You have the opportunity right now to experience yourself on a much deeper level when you let go of the addiction to finger-pointing and embrace the reality, which is that you have created an incredibly complex and beautiful script with deeply, deeply, deeply imagined sets and co-stars and props, and you've laid it all out so that you can wander through it and experience, experience, experience. It's like the greatest carnival ride you can imagine. You created every single bit of it and it's time to revel in it and enjoy the complexity and fascination of it. If it's difficult and painful and hard to deal with, that's interesting, too. That's fascinating, too. And when you're not trying to blame it on someone else and instead take responsibility for it, it will pass very quickly and give you its gift. When you're trying to get rid of it, it's harder for the gift to be given to you.

We walk right now through this field of the fallen. What we see are parts of the journey that are no longer with us. Parts that were left behind, that have been dropped away. You're doing this, too. You walk through your internal battlefield and pieces of you are scattered all over the place. Why? Because those are the parts and pieces of you that you no longer need. They were parts of you that wanted to fight with about what was being created, rather than say, "Yes, yes, yes, I created this. Even this I created." Those parts of you that are defensive, that's a whole battalion. "I got defensive about x, y, z. There's a whole battalion going out onto the field of battle to fight what I think I need to be defensive about. Oh, I was jealous. There goes another battalion. The sniper squad is up there just looking for that one to be jealous about, too." All those low-vibrational states, it's like you're sending out your army. You're sending out your army to go do battle with what? To do battle with your own creation.

You're fighting yourself. This is why we come in and give you all these battle metaphors. Why? To wake you up to the truth that you fight your creation. It's like going to the movies and arguing with what's on the screen. Well, going to the movies is about seeing what's on the screen and interacting with it. You can disagree with it, but standing up in the middle of the movie theater and saying, "Hang on, you're making me defensive," isn't exactly the point. But that's in essence what you're doing all the time. Your creation is being pushed across your screen and you're arguing and defensive and triggered and angry and jealous and you name it 24/7, and what we'd like you to say is: "Wow, wow, wow," the "Wow" opens you to see what's on the screen. Because really, what you see now is a bunch of people fighting.

You fighting yourself is static. It's just like a melee on a battlefield with all the things going on, you can't see the other king. You can't see the other troops. You can't see shit. The way you do this is you focus on interacting with the shit of your static rather than allowing yourself to say yes to it, to manage your triggers, to handle your habits, and to let it all show you its truth. The movie you never see is the beautiful creation you've made, because what you're always seeing is the static going on in front of the screen, the battles going on in front of the screen. You've yet to see the movie but it keeps playing. And the movie, we could say, is your soul's perspective on how Homo sapiens transforms into Homo spiritus. That's what you have the opportunity to experience. That's the gift you're being offered. Every time you don't point your finger, that's one little battle that can poof away and instead be replaced by a glimpse of the movie going by.

Ten

You know we don't particularly have a fondness for royalty. We're not especially fond of people who get to have authority simply by being born. We're sort of more into the idea that your authority comes from being surrounded by people who respect you and will follow you because they respect you. Someone who is simply born hasn't done much, as far as we're concerned. But, every once in a while, one of these types will call us up—that's what you say; we don't have cell phones where we are now, so they tend to ride up on a horse. We've told you about them before. They wear ridiculously impractical clothing and they try to make nice with us. The ironic part of being made nice with by someone sent by someone who is only important because of the way they were born, is that by the time it gets to us, it is so diluted in importance that it is almost not even worth getting up to piss on. But what else are we doing today?

We think we told you that it is our pattern, you may call it a habit, we don't care, your judgments don't trouble us, to take these messenger types and throw them in the creek and roll them around in some dirt. We, of course, don't have to do this. We have many men who respect us who will do it for fun. They roll them around in the dirt, they get rid of all their ridiculous things with flags hanging off of them—try moving through the forest silently with that shit. All that shit has to go. The men roll the messenger types around in the mud. It's entertaining, we'll admit it. Until you've rolled the representation of a person who has authority because of the order in which he was born to a specific person, until you've rolled that person in mud you don't know fun. So, once they've been rolled in mud—and we have to admit sometimes we don't feed them either, we tell them they can eat if they catch their own food; they don't know how—once we have them appropriately dirtied, they'll say something that's supposed to flatter us. One of these types flattering you is the most ridiculous thing. How ridiculous does it have to get? That's pretty fucking ridiculous. He's going to flatter us now, by what? Telling us how cool we are. This is when we typically sharpen things just to see if it'll make him piss. Every once in a while, it does. We consider it a bonus if we make him piss while he's telling us how important we are. That's extra fun.

So, by this time he's dirty and hopefully he's pissed himself and everything's sort of sharp, so it's time to go trudging off to the castle. Or whatever passes for a castle. Let's just use the word castle, why don't we? How often do you get to talk about castles, after all? The interesting bit is that as you're moving back to the castle this person thinks he's in charge. Ha! God, that's a riot. And this is what happens in your life, too. Someone who has some degree of presumed authority has the right to tell you how to be. That's what you do. Now, what we want to say here is this: This presumed authority is fear. In your world, it's fear. In your world, it's fear and habit that have presumed authority in your life. They're just as ridiculous as the messenger of a being that came out of a womb at a specific time in a specific castle to a specific woman who slept with a specific man having any sort of actual authority in your life.

Habit and fear have the same ridiculous nature. They're only there because it's always been that pattern, you see. It's only a pattern that the son of a king has authority and it's only a pattern that fear and habit have authority. It's just a pattern. It's just a pattern. And in our example, you see what we do with him. We take him off his horse, we roll him around in the mud, we don't feed him, and we let him piss himself just for our entertainment. This is the kind of behavior you should have with your fears and your habits. Let them piss themselves for your entertainment. It's not that they really have authority over you. If we weren't interested in tromping off to wherever it is Mr. King wants us to go this time, we'd send the man packing. "Piss off, we're not interested in you." We've done it many times.

You have the same kind of authority over the things that presume to tell you who you are, which are fears and habits, primarily. They presume to tell you who you are. Just like this guy coming on his horse in his silly white clothes wanting to tell us "Oh this, that," and scrape and bow and "You're so important," and this, that and the other crap. We just say, "You're not telling us who we are. Are you kidding? You have no idea who we are. You may have seen some of our actions but that doesn't tell you who we are. You don't know our dreams and passions. You simply have seen actions we've done. Don't presume to know us." You can say the same thing to fear and habit. "Don't presume to know me. Yes, you've been around for a long time. Yes, you've been part of my life. But don't presume to know me. Because I'm connecting to my soul's perspective and am having an experience of the reality of me, and you, fears and habits, don't presume to know me. Don't presume to know me." Do you understand?

So, now that we've had a little bit of teaching, let's talk a bit more just for fun about what happens next. You know you want to get a little bit past the rolling the guy in the dirt and hoping he pisses himself. The ridiculous nature of this being is that he cannot stop being who he is—just like your patterns, right? Even though we've rolled him in mud and made him piss himself and haven't fed him, he still tries to ride his horse with some kind of pride, which is even more ridiculous because the truth of him is not how he rides his horse. The truth of him is who he is inside. But instead of being true to that and saying, "I'm scared," or "Could you please feed me?" or "Jesus, I'm just a person. I have this job but I'm a person, too, and I'd actually like to be able to shit outside of my drawers for once," instead of telling the truth about himself, he tries to pretend and gets to ride his horse in his own excrement. Sitting in your own shit. Sound familiar? Then he smells so bad that we throw him in the river again.

We get to the castle eventually. There are lots of things that happen on the way. Mostly it involves telling him to shut the fuck up—that's the English way of saying it—because habits and fears are noisy, right? So, we ride up to the castle and you have the masses there and the expectation and the fear and the titillation and the envy and the anxiety and the you name it, it's there, because the king has sent for the warriors and they've come out of the forest. This one turns up her nose, that one imagines stealing our purse, and that one over there is starting to look like he might be grow to be a good size after another winter or two. We're keeping an eye on that one.

You are a public figure and all of them are trying to tell you who you are, all of them are giving their impressions of you and again, where are you going to go next? Where are you going to go with that? What are you going to do with that? How do you react? When you arrive at the castle gates after being summoned by the King, the townspeople gather to watch you ride through and all of their fears, their hopes, their passions, their desires, their angers, and their anxieties are projected onto you and it is your choice how to handle it. Your choice how to deal with it. Your choice because you go to see the King.

Eleven

We roll up at the castle, as you might say. We tend to ride horses. You get to the castle and all the people there, if—oh gosh, how would we put it in your terms?—if you ever thought other people could tell you who you are, then rolling up at the castle or maybe showing up on the red carpet at some fancy event would be the place for them to do so. Everyone all lined up deciding who you are for you. *It's not such a good idea to let them.* They can have their own opinions about it, but don't take their opinions as your own. You know who you are. That's the beauty of this entire process. This entire journey is all to help you know who you are, so don't bail out in the middle here as soon as you roll up to the castle with everyone taking pictures of you telling you you're wonderful. In your world they take pictures and they want you to sign autographs and ridiculous, ridiculous, ridiculous. In our world the women give us that look, the men are jealous, for the most part, or afraid, the guards try not to pay so much attention because they're trying to be cool—and we get off the horses and in we go. Always make eye contact with the kid that takes your horse. One, you want to know which one took your horse. Two, you want him to know you know he took your horse, if you know what we mean. We're not sure you have to do this with valets but we think it's probably a good idea, anyway. You want to know who has your ride, as it's said. Those little stable boys are pretty smart, too, so you want to know which one has your horse but you also want to see what kind of a man he might be. We're always on the lookout for new talent. The nice thing about stable boys, they tend to know what's going on, too. Sometimes you can get a little bit of information that is helpful to your cause. Pay attention to everyone. You never know who you might like to talk to again. You've made eye contact with them, they tend to remember you. That and the fact that you outweigh him by 250 pounds. So, off to see the King.

Now, it's really fun to see the King when you stink. Don't let the king's people try to give you a bath before you see the King because it's really fun to watch the King try not to sniff while you're there. We're telling you all the good bits. No one else tells you this stuff, do they? No. When you go see the king, make sure you're smelly and it's good if mud drops off of your clothes. It's good. Why? Because what you want the king to know is that you are not just a little pawn in his game to be manipulated to his benefit, but that you are a person that comes from a society that has values and comes from a culture and a community and tribe and you come into his domain but you do not get converted into him or one like him. Not to say necessarily that being like the king is a bad thing, but it is to say that you want to take the authenticity of you into every encounter. And the authenticity that we present is that we are of the earth and we are of the forest and that we are of the roughness of the world, and to go in front of the king in cleaned-up clothes without our sharp implements would be ridiculous and it would also strip away the truth of who we are. So we recommend that when you go to see the king you take who you are with you, and if that means you drop mud on this perfect floor, well, there you are. You understand? This is very important.

When you go to see the king the thing you have to remember, as well, is that most likely—if you're us, of course; now some other people maybe this doesn't happen to, but we can only speak from our experience—the King is very afraid of you and doesn't want you to know it. You don't get to where we've gotten without knowing when a man is afraid or not. So don't let the King—or in your world, whomever you're encountering, the authority figure that you're encountering—don't let their response to you tell you who you are, either. Sometimes you get a king who thinks he's a badass. In our experience, not all of them are. Every once in a while, you get the experience of one that is actually a badass. Those are the good ones. But when you encounter a king who just thinks he's a badass and he doesn't actually get afraid of you, that one you don't want to work for. Why? Because he's not showing you his true nature. We would rather work for a king who's afraid than work for one who's trying to pretend he's not. When you are encountering people who know who they are and present themselves authentically—whether it's a king or a boss or a baker—you can trust the exchange to be high-vibrational or at least conscious or at least not generating more static. So, when you go to see the king, whoever the king is in your world, if you show up authentically you've done your part to contribute to a conscious conversation. If they don't do their half, well, that's something very, very important to know immediately. And occasionally it is worth the journey.

In this case, in this time, in this example, in this story of going to see the King, we have a good one here, although a good king is not necessarily the highest type of person on our list. But in this case, we have a story about a king that we were relatively pleased to go see. We'd had good relations with this one before. Keeps his word. He doesn't get all pissy that we bring our truth, which means mud, into his hall. He doesn't require a whole bunch of bowing and scraping in order to not feel afraid of us. When they ask you to go against your nature in order for them to be comfortable, you should be wary. Whoever it is you're dealing with, if they do not like to be around your true self, you want to know that. The only way you'll know it is if you take your true self into the encounter. This is important stuff all mixed into a fairytale, but it's still important. All right. So, off you go. Here's the king. This king is the kind of king who says, "Oh, we're happy to see you and your men and we want you well fed," and doesn't make any comments about the fact that he also hopes that we take a bath or two. He sends the men off to be entertained and fed and he wants to speak to us alone. This is a good king. Do you know how you know? Because he doesn't need to grandstand in front of all in order to feel secure in himself. He doesn't need everyone to see his authority in order to feel that he has authority in the dynamic, and he wants to sit down and look eye-to-eye and discuss something rather than just dispense orders. You want to be like this king in this way.

So, we go and we sit with the king in this little side area he has there and his nice women bring us nice food and because we know this hall, we have already sent our lieutenant around to, let's just say, remove the one spying on the side there. You can imagine hearing the sounds of a little scuffle off to the side and the king gives a wry little smile because one, he didn't know you knew about that spot and two, he knows he's called the right person. Why? Because he sees that we're aware of our environment. When you bring your complete self to an exchange, you need to also be aware of the environment you're in. As you bring your complete self, you expand into and start to incorporate more of the world you walk in. Your complete self has the ability to experience more without triggering the survival instinct. The narrow self wants the world to be narrow so that the threats are limited. That's what the survival instinct says. The complete self starts to expand into a greater picture, so as you experience life as your complete self you experience more of your surroundings, too. This will be a beautiful exploration for you.

Anyway, what does the king want? The king says that some folks are coming for a visit. Some neighboring-kingdom folks are coming for a visit. They're going to come in a boat. And when they arrive on the shore of his land, he would like to have a show of muscle be present beside him. Now, of course, the king has all kinds of soldiers and men that ride horses and this, that, and the other thing. But the king knows that this other group of people respect men of character. And the king knows that this other group of people are going to be pleased to see a reflection of themselves present in his kingdom. Because the king knows that his court is like the courts of all kingdoms, more about the politics and the presentation than about the presence, he would like us to sort of stand next to him and be authentic. What do you call it? Emanate your true self.

Well now, this is what we call an easy job. And we'll do this for this king on one condition. We'll do this for the king on the condition that the king also emanates his complete self. Because we don't get into agreements that are half-assed. If the king wants us to be true then we're asking the king to show up with truth, as well. Now, this is challenging because he wants to play politics and he was hoping he could slough off the job of being the complete self to someone else. You can't give away that job and that's the moral of this section of our story. You can't give away the job of being your complete self. There's nothing that substitutes for being your authentic self. We don't suggest trying to be it sometimes and not trying to be it other times. The king can look us in the eye in this moment, but he doesn't want to take that truth of him into this encounter—even knowing that the other people value that kind of honesty. Why? Because of vulnerability. It feels weak to be that exposed, but we know that the only place of true strength is when you're vulnerable enough to be the truth of you. So, we say we'll stand beside the king but we won't put up with any petty bullshit. We will walk at the first sign that he's using us, in essence, to give him street-cred. Because an easy job is easy, but a job that compromises who we are is not worth it—and that's another thing for you to take with you. Compromising who you are is never worth it. It never pays. It never turns out. And it's hard on the physical body.

The king is afraid of us because we come as our true selves and the king honors us because we come as our true selves, and neither one of his states of being influences us much. It's nice to sleep in his hall and to eat his good food and to look at his beautiful women and, yes, to occasionally take a bath. But none of that can be done under the guise of the king telling us who we are. It is us being true to us in his hall. This is how to go out into your workplace, go out into your workplace and be yourself in their hall. No one tells you who you are.

You are your true self regardless of your circumstance and you do not let others, no matter how much they would ply you with compliments and beautiful women, tell you who you are. Knowing who you are and emanating your complete self is the fabric of your being. Releasing that truth to anyone else's power is slavery, energetic slavery. The only one holding those bonds on you in that energetic slavery is you. You have the key. You have the key and you have the bonds and you make the choice.

Twelve

The king wants us to go off and do something with him and we said, "Why not?" So that evening, we did take a bath. It's not like we don't like to bathe, we enjoy bathing. We just don't want to bathe in order to be someone we're not. It's time to have a bath, why not? And it's nice to bathe at the castle. Why? Because when you bathe at the castle the water is warm. When you bathe in the forest the water is cold, hence, a reason to bathe at the castle. You can be tough all you want but it is nice every once in a while to be kind to your body, yes?

So, off we go to sit in the tub with the beautiful young women—don't call us sexist, it doesn't exist in our time. Beautiful young women filled the tub and we got in. And because we don't have to stand with the king on the shore of the ocean until tomorrow, we even had something to drink. We made merry, as you like to say.

If the king wants you to do something for him, you may as well take advantage of the comforts while you're about it. So off we go. The nice thing is that in the castle, there are just so many people that have jobs looking after people. They're everywhere. They look after you and they clean things up. There're certain things they don't get to do, like touch anything that's sharp. If they want to clean mud off of this, that, or the other thing they can do that. It's nice because we're not unknown at the castle, so sometimes when we come around, well let's just say it's nice when somebody mends your things. We can certainly mend our own things but it's nice when someone else does it. Every once in a while there's a little something extra added in and we enjoy that, too. There is something nice about fresh, what would you call them? You know the things you wear under, it's nice when your unders are nice and new and clean. And if they smell pretty like roses, well, it helps you remember that you're not alone in this world.

The king is asking us to show up now so we've gotten ourselves together and we're going down to stand along the shore and see who's coming to visit. They come along and yes, they're big and shining and blondish, and they have beautiful boats. They bristle and we bristle and the king talks and the other king talks, and it's all good. The king is authentic enough to make the thing all work out and we decide to have games. Now, you like to have games, we know you play games. You play games of chance and you play games of skill and you play games just for fun and you run about and exercise your muscles because it feels damn good to do so. This is a normal act of being human. But again, no matter what happens in any of these environments and whether these games extend to the games of corporate giants, or the games extend to Monopoly with your kids, there's a point at which you have to ask, "Is winning this game telling me who I am? Is how I'm playing the game telling me who I am? Or am I knowing myself regardless?"

There's sense in you that you have to accomplish in order to know yourself. There's a sense in you that you have to achieve in order to know yourself. Your society is based on rewarding the victor and indicating your worth, indicating your nature by your accomplishments, by your résumé. You're promoted at work when you do well, et cetera. You're paid bonuses if things go your way. What happens is that you only feel accomplished if you make accomplishments based on other's standards. You must not fall into the trap that says: "I am only me if I'm accomplishing based on another's standards. I'm only me when I compare myself to another's standards. I'm only me if…." There's no such thing as: "I'm only me if…." That's just crap. "I am always me, regardless," is the position we'd like you to adopt. You are you if you stand on the sidelines, you are you if you compete, you're you if you are the victor, you are you if you are the vanquished. You are you, regardless, and as you bring your complete self into all these interactions, it allows you to emanate the truth of you and to show those you interact with, regardless of what form you interact with them, to show them that you are the truth of you. This is how they know your nature. You've heard the saying: No one likes a sore loser. Of course no one does, and no one likes too much of a braggart for a winner, either. Humility is respected on some level. We don't particularly care for it. We're not into humility, we're not into bragging. We're not into being sore losers. What we're into is a consistent emanation of our truth, regardless of the circumstances in which we find ourselves. And this is what we invite you to do, too. Consistently emanate the truth of you regardless of the circumstances; choose your reaction based on your higher-vibrational, conscious experience of yourself.

So, you wrestle and you're vanquished and you smile and laugh and pat the other one on the back and you thank him for a well-fought match. You wrestle and you're the victor and you do the same thing, and by your consistency they will know you. By your consistency you will know yourself. By your consistency, when you compare you to you, you can really see progress, because you're consistently showing the completeness of you regardless of the circumstances you find yourself in. You will sense progress in the process.

The greatest gift you can give to yourself is to be consistent regardless of the circumstances you find yourself in. This doesn't mean the same, this means consistent, whether you're the victor or the vanquished you still act the same. When you roll the dice and they roll in the direction you hoped they'd roll or in the direction that you didn't hope they'd roll, you react the same.

Not because you're faking it but because anything that is presenting itself to you is presenting itself to you for growth. It's how you react to it that dictates the growth you get out of it, not the result of the action. The result of the action does not give you growth, it's the *reaction* to the experience that gives you growth. *That's* the gift you give yourself.

One of these men on the other side—let's call him Eric—Eric has a proposition. He would like us to come along with him on a little adventure. One of these "Let's just go and rape and pillage" kind of things—for the fun of it, he says. He doesn't use the word "fun," but it's the best translation we have. "Let's go rape and pillage for the fun of it" is basically what he's offering, to shortcut the whole thing. In the moment of making this proposal, we're sitting around and there's much merriment after the games of the day, much drinking and eating, beautiful women, the fire's roaring. You can imagine the picture, we believe.

Eric calls us out, in essence, in front of everyone. He says, "Come, let us go together, now that we've become friends and brothers, let us go together to see this other neighbor and take what is theirs." It happens, right? We're looking around and we're thinking, "Well, we have it pretty good now, and we've had it pretty good in the forest, and we had it pretty good before we were in the forest. We're not really feeling like we need any pillaging because we can't really carry any more sharp things, and we have a new pair of underwear from the gal last night, and things are pretty flush in our book. Especially when you have to carry everything you want, you don't want too many things. The old horse can only carry so much after we get on it, right? So, there he is and he's now standing and asking us, "Come with us, we'll go together, we can leave on the tide," and all that crap—you've seen it in movies, you know what it's like.

All our men have started to bristle now, because they know the truth. The truth being that conquering does not conquer the self. Just like you going out and getting a promotion does not make you a better person. You piling up a bunch of money doesn't give you ascension, right? Money is not rare. Consciousness, ascension, Homo spiritus—those are rare things; money's not rare, but he's calling us out. All of his men are making hoopla about the whole thing, and all of our men are starting to slowly slide their knives out from under the table, because it may come to that, it may have to come to that.

Thirteen

Eric stands up. The splashing of the ale is almost obligatory when challenging other warriors to come pillage with you. So, we're here at the table and we have our arms here and we're eating the food and he stands up and makes this grand pronouncement blah, blah, blah. And the king is here. We sit just to the right of the king, of course, and the king is noticeably tense, let's call it, because he's invested in the projection of what's going to happen. Mr. King doesn't spend much time in the moment, we'll tell you that right now. So we're there, we're eating, Eric is doing his splashing-of-ale challenge. The men, if you could see under the table, have all pulled knives because they know it's best to be ready. Because this may not go exactly the way other people would like.

We take a moment. They're all exuberant you know, because they're drunk and excited and blood-thirsty, and they want to go pillage. And we sit; we sit with their challenge. Let's not kid ourselves, that's exactly what it is. It's one thing to play dice and cards and wrestle, it's quite another thing to prove yourself on the field of battle or field of pillage. They want to measure themselves as comrades. Who knows? They might turn on us there. Couldn't say. We haven't actually made real good friends with them yet.

We sit there and we just wait. And the king gets more tense and the men continue to eat, but we know they're ready. We've been here before. Eric and his friends were kind of hollering and hooting and now they're growing quiet. All the servants have gone quiet and you can hear the crackle of the fireplace, and a dog or two snuffles and resituates itself, but the tension in the room grows thicker and thicker and thicker. And then we look up from our meal. We look directly into Eric's eyes and we hold his gaze and then we say, "No" and look back down at our meal. To this, of course, there is shock, and the king gets more fidgety, and Eric starts boasting.

You don't let them tell you who you are, ever. No one can tell you who you are. Keep that in mind. Now they're going to start goading us. "What, aren't you strong enough, aren't you brave enough, don't you think…?" All that stuff. The temptation is to defend yourself. Of course, we're not at fisticuffs yet. Hopefully we won't get there, but we might. The temptation for you, when you're in a similar situation, is to start to do your but-and-because thing. To defend yourself, to justify your position, to explain it, to try and win them over to your side. We couldn't give a shit whether Eric and his buddies are on our side—because you have to remember, we don't have a side. We have our understanding of ourselves. Not their projection of who we are. You get it?

Eric continues his boasting and we continue to eat because, after all, part of going to see the king is that the food's good and you don't have to kill it yourself, nor do you have to cook it. We suggest, when you go to see the king, you take advantage of this fact. Eric now has worked himself up. His face is so red, he's just so furious about something. We know what he's furious about: He's furious with the fact, unconscious as it may be, that his manhood is in question now. Because he's used to expressing his manhood by going out and walking all over other people. We're expressing our manhood by sitting in our own energy. We don't need conquering to prove who we are. He feels like he does. So now we're at odds; we weren't at odds until this moment. At this moment, we're at odds because now he doesn't see us as someone who's like him, and that's when he's most dangerous. He may need for us to be like him in order to be comfortable in our presence. The king is shitting his pants. Not literally, but close, because he sees this whole thing falling apart now. Because we are going to be true to what's true to us rather than go along with what this guy has dreamed up.

It's interesting when you're in a situation like this where someone else's knowing of themselves is so predicated on others' actions. There's not a lot you can do but be the example of the truth of you to them. Now, we're going to give Eric a back door, we're going to give Eric another choice. Why? Because we don't want to have to kill the guy. The king certainly doesn't want us to kill the guy, and as you go out into the world emanating your truth, you emanate your truth simply by being you. You show people there are other options by emanating your truth and being you, right? So we're going to give Eric another option and we say to him, "You don't want to go there. You don't want to go there this time of year, you don't want to go there," whatever reason we think of. We just think something up, in the moment, it doesn't matter what.

Not why we don't want to go there. Why we don't want to go there is because we're not into it. If we say, "You don't want to go there this time of year," then he has a back door. He has a way to save face and say, "Oh, you're right, the heat of the moment came upon me." He's young, he may not take the back door, so we're going to give him another one. "You don't want to go there, stay here with us and we'll do some kind of exercise." We'll dream something up. And in your world, as you experience people like this, whose opinions of themselves are based on how *you* act, the best thing you can do is emanate the truth of you and give them options if it's coming to a head. When you are faced with someone who wants *their* opinion of you to be *your* opinion of you, you are most challenged to emanate the truth of you. In that moment, when you emanate the truth of you, "No" is a complete statement. It's a complete sentence. It doesn't need to be defended, but you can present options to them for making different choices.

So in our story we're going to let Eric say he took the back door, because if he doesn't take the back door, the story ends really quickly. Our guys jump up over the table, kill his guys, it's over. That's not a very fun story. Plus, there's a lot to clean-up, and we're wearing our new underwear. We're not really in the mood to get it all bloody, so there you go. Plus, then the king shits his pants and then we have to leave the castle, and actually we were sort of hoping to sleep in that bed because we kind of like the looks of that girl over there, and that's just the honest truth. So we're moving the story along in the direction that feels good to us. What do you think of that for creating your reality?

Eric decides, "Oh yeah, you're right." Then he flatters us, "The wisdom of the king's men." Then he expects us, again, expects us to be who *he* thinks we are, or to respond to *his* impression of us. This is something you have to get into your systems. You can enjoy flattery but don't let it tell you who you are, just as you can experience disparagement but not let it tell you who you are. You know you better than anyone else can know you. He flatters us and tells us, "Oh the king's men are so smart, so wise, we shall stay here and on the morrow we shall go hunt something."

Better hunting it than hunting each other. That's the way we look at it.

The thing about this story that we want you to really settle in with is that we emanated our truth in the moment and we held to what we knew was true. We did not extrapolate into the past or the future. We did not get emotional. The feelings of the moment were, "We're not interested in pillaging, we're certainly not interested in going anywhere with these guys," and we are not afraid in that position, come what may.

Now, the boys all took out their knives—why? Because you have your tools ready when you have this kind of circumstance, because you are rubbing up against unconsciousness. The best tool to have at hand when rubbing up against unconsciousness is consciousness. In this case, our tools are sharp and pointy, but your tools are just as effective.

So we're off on the hunt the next day, and at this point in the story we're going to bring in Eric wanting to be more conscious, OK? So, the hunt is going on and the men are having a great time and we don't know what we're after, say boar, it's always a good one because they're dangerous—very, very dangerous. Eric comes beside us as we watch the men run and do their thing and says, "I thought it might come to blades last night." Our response, "If it had, we would have killed you without a thought." There's the truth. Because what he's saying is: "I thought I was going to be unconscious," and you say, "My consciousness would have put that down." You see? He says, "I know that would have happened, I agree with you that that would have been the case."

In our land, men are not known for their steady minds, they're only known for their bravery. Bravery's another word for unconscious, bravery's another word for: "I'll just do it and see what happens. I'll go with the flow of my emotions, I'll just run in." Courage is feeling the fear and doing it anyway. Bravery is just cannon fodder, a lot of the time. That's the discernment between the two terms; not everyone defines them that way but that's how we define them. It's interesting to have brave fellows around; every now and again they live through it and they typically have good stories, but we'd rather have a bunch of courageous men by our side than 100 brave ones. Bravery's overrated, in our book.

Fourteen

Considering that they had first wanted to go and rape and pillage the neighbors, we think that Eric and his men wanting to hang out with us is a good outcome. *Emanating the truth and speaking up allowed for a different alternative to present itself.*

Now, some might think, "Oh God, now you're stuck with Eric and his band of marauders." Eric and the Marauders. That might make a good band name. Eric and the Marauders—oh, the potential.

So, Eric and the marauders, because now we have to call them that, because it's too cute to pass up, want to join our band. Now, you have to remember that we are not that many in this story. In this story, we are twelve or so, we are not a huge group of men. But Eric and the marauders want to join in, and the thing about Eric and the marauders is that they are almost equal to us in number. That immediately causes a little bit of a thing. Because when you have equal numbers it's very easy to believe that you have equal representation of how the group will be led. Eric and the marauders are coming along because Eric is all keen to see what we know, but his marauders are a little confused as to why he would make himself subordinate to us. Why he would put himself in a position of less authority. His men are confused by this. Now, because Eric is just a kid in his spiritual world, he doesn't tell them, he just expects that, because he's made the decision, they'll follow along with no problem.

Now, this isn't the army. This isn't something where someone gives you an order and you just obey it. We're twenty guys walking through the forest.

Let's be real. The only hierarchy that's happening is the one that's created from respect or fear, or both. Eric didn't take his marauder's opinions into account much when he took them off of their boat and fed them for a while and now wants them to go through the forest with us.

What's interesting here is Eric, well, he didn't tell us that he didn't talk to his men, but we could see it and we knew that it was going to brew. We knew there was going to be a problem because you have to remember, just before Eric decided to join our band, what were we doing? We were competing in games of chance and other things, right? So Eric's men knew that our men had a cohesiveness. Our group had an unwritten structure to it. His group was far more "Do as I say." They did not gel very well with our group because the leadership styles were so different. They kept looking for guidance. Eric kept saying, "We're going to go this way," not explaining. We don't have to explain anything. They're not our guys, anyway, and we don't know them. We're not going to bother to get to know them until we get to know them, if you know what we mean.

It was not pretty when it came to an end because the men got hot-headed. They grumbled and they did not want to play nice. They started to feel betrayed by Eric, they started to feel misled. They started to feel like, "When are we ever going to go home, why are we here, what are we doing?" Those are emotions. The actual feeling was simply, "What the fuck?" But instead of that, they went with all those other things we described. Eric could have simply stepped in and said, "Look, we need to do this for a little while," but he didn't. He didn't, he didn't, he didn't. He didn't until one day, when we were off doing something important and not all of his guys decided to help. It wasn't pretty for them.

The result is that the emotions kept them from having an experience of camaraderie, which is one of the reasons they came along with us in the first place. It denied them the opportunity to learn, which is another reason they came along with us. And it created a situation where a couple of people didn't quite live after that. Oops. Which sort of pissed off the rest of them, we have to say.

Now, we didn't kill them. We were just doing something. We had a job to do and they were supposed to help and they didn't do a very good job of helping. And that's what happened. The moral of the story is: Tell the truth. Part of the reason Eric couldn't tell his men what was going on was that he didn't want to admit he didn't know everything. He didn't want to admit that there was something for him to learn. He didn't want to admit that, and because he didn't want to admit that, he denied them the opportunity to have authentic presence in the band; an authentic presence with us. It cost two of them their lives. Now, Eric is even further diminished in the hierarchy of the no-hierarchy of our experience. He's even more diminished in their viewpoint because they've lost two of their comrades. And they're still wandering around the woods wondering, "What the fuck?"

The opportunity here is to remember, you don't want to be an Eric wandering in the woods, not admitting to yourself that you want what's being offered. You see, there's that part of you that will sometimes say, "I want something but I don't want to admit I want it." Again, it falls back into the weakness/vulnerability thing. I'm in a position of weakness or I'm in a position of vulnerability. Vulnerability is based in truth. Weakness is based in lying. "I don't want anyone to know I need to learn something, therefore, I'm going to be in a position of weakness" rather than admit there's something to learn. "We're going to go with them, and yes, they're going to be in charge of what we do." Eric went into weakness and didn't inform his men.

He was a mess. He was a mess. You might say, "Well, why didn't you step in and tell him how to be?" Well, it's the same reason you're not advised to run around shaking shoulders and demanding people behave in a certain way. The truth of the matter is, you have knowledge and people will come to you if it's your turn to share it with them. After this little mishap, Eric did not come to us, but his men did. One by one, here and there, and they said, "We don't want him to lead us anymore." Some of them didn't want to be there, some of them wanted to come with us. Until finally, Eric isolated himself through his own inability to tell the truth about the situation he found himself in. Through his own inability to discern what was going on with him. Through his own inability to offer his truth to the situation, he ended up isolating himself.

Don't be an Eric. Be vulnerable. Tell the truth. Be honest about your feelings. Be willing. Be willing to admit when you want to learn something. Open to the fact that you don't know everything. And allow. Allow yourself to be in the presence and the moment of the situation at hand. That's it.

Fifteen

What is Eric going to do now? His men have lost confidence in him. His men are confused. "Why are we tromping around in the woods with these strangers when we could be going home to our sweethearts? Why are we tromping around in the woods with these strangers who seem to know what they're doing so much better than the guy we're here with? What are we doing? Why are we here? What is going on?" These are questions you've asked yourself many times, and just as the men look externally of themselves to Eric for the answers, we see you doing that, too. You look outside of yourself, saying, "Why am I here?" You're asking the wrong person. It's not: "Why am I here with him?" It's: "Why am I here now? Who am I? Who am I and why am I having this experience? Do I want it to change and, if so, let's get on with the business of changing."

Back to Eric. He's a bit young. We don't know if we ever told you that, but he's a bit young for his position. His men are more experienced. He has got some kind of royalty in his blood, we're sure of it. He has got some: "I can be in charge because I'm the son of the king" kind of energy that he runs, and his men are like: "I am here because I've been here my whole life." The men would like to be in a position where they can respect their leader. Their leader would like to be in a position where he's respected by the men. This is not what's happening currently.

Some of the men have come to us now. They've come to us and said, "OK, this is the deal. We are not happy. We either want to be with you or we want to go home. We don't want to be in this limbo-land you have us stuck in." We say, of course, "We don't have you stuck in any damn thing. Walk away if you wish." Then here it comes—and you do this one, too—"but how would I? But what would happen? But what would be the consequences?" But, but, but, but, fucking but. Geez, if we hear that word one more time we think we will have to stab someone. But, but, but, but, what? What is it that you want? What are you doing to bring that into your life? Are you willing to face the consequences of your desires being made manifest? Those desires may be that you get more money, that you have a better position, that you have a husband, a wife, a kid, whatever, but are you willing to deal with what happens to you when you do? By deal with it, we mean being happy for once. We mean stepping into the world in a way that allows you to know yourself.

You see, we look at Eric's men and we say: What is in your way? And we look at you and we say: What is in your way? What is in your way of being the truth of you? Just like we look at them and say: What is in your way of being the truth of you? "Well, I've sworn allegiance to Eric." Well, then, why are you talking to us? If you've made the choice to swear allegiance to Eric, you're not being very allegiant right now. You're blowing it already. You may as well stop blowing it and get what you want instead. You're afraid to change but you're already sneaking around the outside of change in an unconscious and rather unattractive way. Change or don't change. "Well, I can't break my allegiance." This is the one we're going to stab. If the urge comes upon us and we can't hold back, we've already picked out the one we want. That one. That one that keeps repeating: "I've sworn allegiance. I can't leave him but I don't want to be with him." Sounds like some of your relationships. "But I'm married to him. We live in the same house. I love him." Yeah, you love him. Why are you talking to us again?

Back to Eric. His men are all in various stages of disruption. You have grizzled veterans that feel, "This is the one that's going to get me killed," and you have the younger ones that feel, "This isn't nearly as much fun as I thought it was going to be." You have the other ones who feel, "Can I just go home now?" And then there's Eric. Eric has come to us. God, he's pissed. Shit. Maybe we should stab him, instead. He's mad at us because he thinks we're trying to steal his men. Yeah, we want the one that's sworn allegiance to you but is backstabbing you. That's the one we want. Please give him to us. Yeah, right. We're tempted to stab him. Stand close to each other and we'll get both of you with one go.

We're just listening. You have to remember that we've been as a little band here for a very long time, and so the men, our men, are starting to realize where things are headed. What's really interesting about the guys that have been around with us for a while is they'll do very interesting things. Like all of a sudden in this conversation, everyone needs to sharpen their knife at the same time. You see, sharpening your knife gives you a very, very good reason to have your knife out. Do you understand? Because as fast as we are, it's always very nice for it to start in your hand. So, all of a sudden, everyone just feels the urge to sharpen something. It makes a nice soundtrack for the conversation with Eric. Eric is mad because he thinks we're trying to steal his men. And we say: Eric, you can leave anytime you want. This is the other thing you do. You get into a path and you forget you have choice. You do this at your jobs a lot. You start to want to buck the system and you start to resent the system and you start to resent your coworkers and you start to resent the environment you're in, and all the while we're going: Quit, quit, quit. Just leave. If it's that bad, why are you still there? Why have you decided that you have to fight in that environment? Why can't you just walk away? We say to old Eric: Just leave. "No, no, no. I don't want to leave." Why don't you want to leave? "Because I still think there's more for me to learn here." Yes, learning that you can leave is probably at the top of the list.

So, we tell Eric: Look Eric, this is the deal. We don't want your men. We're not trying to steal them. We brought you along because you wanted to come. You bitch about what's actually happening, and you have every opportunity to leave at any time. Then the conversation's over. See, we don't have to justify our position. Do you justify your position? Yup. Remember, "No" is a complete statement. You might want to put a period on there just for fun but " 'N' 'O' period" is a complete sentence. You don't have to justify the decisions you make. We are not going to beg Eric to stick around. We are not going to diffuse his anxiety about the fact that we're stealing his men. We're not going to puff him up to try to make him feel better about himself. The bottom line: Eric, make your choice. You came here to learn or you came here to leave. Do what you want to do. We don't care. That's one of the hardest things for you to hear: "I don't care what you do." But the truth is if you care about yourself first, you don't need other people to care about you, for you to know who you are. Eric doesn't know who he is and he thought tromping around with us would teach it to him. The bottom line is, what he's learning is that he doesn't like who he is, but he hasn't yet gotten to the point where he knows how to handle that.

Eric decides to stay and we are going to do mad scientist on Eric. We are going to take the fact that we know Eric and we know his men and we are going to mix up the dynamic a little bit. Because since Eric decided to stay, it's no longer Eric in charge of his boys and us in charge of our boys. We're in charge of all of it. Suck it up, Eric. Let's see what Eric thinks of that.

We always reserve the right to stab him. We keep a special sword just for the ones who are really annoying. We have hope for old Eric, just like we have hope for you. Eric, unfortunately, isn't as advanced as your left toe. We'll hopefully be able to boost him up a little without having to go into service, but he might not like what we're going to do next. We think he has some time of not liking it coming. But sometimes you learn to like things you didn't like at first.

Sixteen

Let's be clear. The chances of us stabbing Eric are about zero. The desire to stab Eric is about 95 percent. Let's be clear. There is a difference between those two conditions. We can want to stab Eric a lot without actually ever doing it. We're not going to waste Eric. There's hope for him. So, Eric is whining and the men are sharpening their knives. Yes, we can hear them sharpening their knives.

Have you ever seen a 250 pound man pick his teeth with a freshly sharpened knife? It will scare you if you aren't used to it, we would imagine. This one over here, he's especially fond of doing that. He gets kind of disgusting about it, too. There's this flicking thing he likes to do. It's all intimidation. It's disgusting. We even think it's disgusting, and it takes a lot to disgust us. But it's all intimidation. It's all showing up and saying: "Look, do you really, truly, truly, truly want to change the dynamic we're experiencing?" We would like you to not be disgusting, but to be more in that perspective. More in that perspective of having that sense of self so firmly rooted that when someone comes into your environment and tries to tell you who you are, that it's: "You really want to change this dynamic between us?" It's not a sense of: "You don't want to mess with me," because unless you are a martial arts master or weapons master or any of that stuff, you can't really pull off the "You don't want to mess with me" thing. You're not exactly geared for that in this incarnation. But there's a sense of saying energetically, "Do you really want to shift the dynamic between us?" And that's what we'd like to see you get more familiar with. Your ability to be conscious and understand yourself, your ability to sit in vulnerability rather than weakness, your ability to bring in your soul's perspective makes you a very powerful force and that powerful force doesn't have to be a martial arts master in order for other people to be alerted that they're in a situation, a dynamic, that can be uncomfortable for them.

How many times have you asked someone to be conscious and they haven't been able to? That's the same thing as flicking your teeth with your knife and all that. It's your version of it. It's your version of saying, "I am willing to step forward and be conscious in this moment. I am willing to tell the truth. I am willing to be vulnerable. I'm willing to show up as my complete self. I'm willing to access my soul's perspective. Are you willing to meet me in that? If you're not, you need to step back. You need to step off. Because that's where I'm coming from." In essence, that's bringing all these tools and all these men that are doing their various knife sharpening with you to the interaction that you find yourself in. Whether it's with a husband, a boyfriend, a sister, a sibling, whatever. It's not an aggressive stance. You're not being aggressive. Our teeth-picking man is not being aggressive. All he's doing is picking his teeth with a sharp knife. But what he's saying is: "At any minute, this can change," and what we would like you to know is that at any minute you can take it into even more consciousness. Any conversation you're in can go even more conscious. You can drop into the moment even more deeply. That is your version of, in essence, calling someone out because you're going to where your tools are. You're going from relaxing by the campfire to immediate readiness for attentiveness to the situation.

When we encounter Eric and he's whining, what he's whining about is unconsciousness. What he's whining about are fears and certainties. What he's whining about is puffed-up pride. What he's whining about is jealousy. None of this is conscious. If we speak to Eric in an incredibly conscious way he will either run or fight. Or be conscious back. See, there's fight-or-flight or consciousness, and we don't know which one Eric is going to choose. On some level, letting the men do their thing with their knives puts Eric in a position where he needs to choose between fight-or-flight. It's our role as a leader to bring in the option of being conscious. You don't have to deal only on the level of fight-or-flight. Take the leadership role and bring in the option of consciousness as well. The consciousness starts with you telling the truth about you.

So, here we go. Eric is whining. So we say Eric, "What is it that you're truly afraid of?" Now when you ask a question you should be prepared to answer the same question yourself. That's consciousness. If he said something like, "Well, what are you truly afraid of?" we could tell him our truth. Our truth is that we're afraid of living an unconscious life. That's our greatest fear; that we would slip into unconsciousness at some point. Not losing consciousness as in collapsed, but into unconscious behaviors. That we would walk the planet in an unconscious way, that's our greatest fear. Therefore, we bring sand paper, Eric, script holder, Eric, into our life. Eric's unconscious acts give us an opportunity to examine our conscious walk. See how that works? We say, "Eric, that's our greatest fear, what's yours?"

Eric's greatest fear is that he will not be seen as valuable. "I'm afraid I'm not valuable to others." Well, once again, if your greatest fear has to do with other people's perspective of you, you need to revise your greatest fear because you cannot change other people's perspective of you. If you fear their perspective, then you're setting yourself up for a life of fear. We explain this to Eric and he says, "Well, I guess then my greatest fear is that I won't respect my own path. I won't respect the path I've walked. When I become an old man, I'll look back with regret about the path I walked." OK, now we're getting down to it. He's afraid that he will regret the path he's walked and he's living where? He's living from that fear.

You do this. You live from fear, rather than letting fear inform you of an opportunity to be conscious. Becoming conscious of your fear doesn't immediately take away the physical response to it in all instances. When you become aware of your fears you tend to think something is wrong which can't be fixed. This is the moment you need to remind yourself, "That's right, this is my body and I am not my body. I am my soul's perspective experiencing the physical form. Using spiritual discipline I can override and transform the body's interaction with the survival instinct." Additional consciousness about the fear will allow your body to abate the adrenaline response. This is the Warrior's Path.

The warrior transforms his or her reaction to the survival instinct in order to bring the moment into focus without the distractions of the past or the future, without the distractions of the survival instinct and without the distractions of other people's opinions, whether they be king or page. That's what the warrior does. That's what the self-possessed conscious human does. You walk in the world from your soul's perspective. Not from the perspective of others.

Seventeen

We don't know about you, but we're kind of bored with Eric. Eric is just boring us. Let's say Eric chooses to go. Can we just get rid of Eric? Because we were going to stab him, and then we decided not to and then he just whined so much. You see you get to read the story but we have to watch it, too, and if there is anything worse than listening to someone whine, it's watching them whine. Oh, and the men are sick of Eric, too. OK, so Eric decides to go. We're just getting rid of him. Eric as a plot device has been used up. Isn't it great to be the author of the story? Troublesome characters can just go.

Eric decides to go back home. Not all of Eric's men want to go with him. What are we going to do with the rest of them? Some of them we actually think are good men and the ones that didn't whine about the whole thing, we're going to keep. But there are two or three, especially that one who didn't want to forsake, that one, he's got to go, or we're going to have to stab him for sure. So, off he goes. Most of them go with Eric. We keep four.

We have these four guys that are left. We'll call them 1, 2, 3, and 4 until we bother learning their names. 1, 2, 3, and 4 have proven themselves to be adequate warriors. They've proven themselves to be adequate in the field. They know how to take care of themselves. They're relatively quiet when we walk, et cetera. The problem is that they are not used to our terrain. Eric's land is different than ours. We are mostly in a deep-forest-kind of an environment. They are used to a more open kind of a field, you might call it a savanna kind of an environment, whereas our environment is much, much more wooded. The problem with this is they are not used to traveling silently. They are not used to traveling with the environment they're in. Therefore, they kind of bumble about more than they like. Thus, they are having a hard time loving themselves. They are out of their environment and having a hard time loving themselves. Feel a little familiar?

As they move through the environment where they have a hard time appreciating and loving themselves, they start to feel less and less and less skilled. Now, we don't need four extra guys. We only kept these guys around because we can tell, despite their lack of familiarity with the environment, that they have skills and that they could become valuable members of our band. We are not judging them. We are certainly correcting them. We're certainly letting them know where they could improve. We're certainly pointing out where they almost got us killed. But we are not judging them. You see, this is what we wish for you. You can find places within yourself where you would like to change but you don't need to judge yourself in order to bring those to the light of day. We can say, "Look, 3, if you step on a dry branch again we're going to stab you." This isn't judging him that he's an idiot for stepping on a dry branch. This is simply saying that stepping on dry branches isn't appropriate. We're not thinking he's an idiot. We're thinking he needs to learn quickly so he doesn't get everyone killed. We're telling him: This is what you need in order to function in this environment. We're not saying: You, as a being, suck.

What happens when you get into a foreign environment is you start to judge yourself. Then, people give you feedback and you judge the feedback instead of saying, "I don't know anything." This is where "I don't know anything" comes to hand. If 1, 2, 3, and 4 could relax into "I don't know anything" and let themselves believe that they wouldn't be with us unless there was a place for them and relax into learning rather than asserting, they would have an opportunity to meld with our group much more quickly. The ones that resist and want to prove themselves rather than allow themselves to be receptive are the ones that we're going to have to get rid of—1 and 4 are looking like they're failing in that department; 2, he's OK; 3, well, let's just say he spent too much time with Eric and leave it at that.

Imagine yourself a stranger in a strange land, not a hard stretch. You feel that way frequently. As you walk through this strange land you find yourself in, even if it's simply your own life that's expanded, as you walk through the strange life you're in, one, don't forget the skills you already have. Don't forget your tools that you already carry with you, but don't fall back on: "I already know all the answers. I'm going to cram this new experience into my old way of being, my old way of seeing." Stay open with: "I don't know anything about now, but I know what I bring to now." You don't come into the now as a babe fresh out of the womb. You come into the now with the collection of yourself. The best you can do is to be in the now from an open and receptive position that allows you to evaluate and interact with the experience as it unfolds.

You can plan ahead to be in battle, but you never can know precisely how it will go. The most valuable assets of a warrior are being able to think on your feet, evaluate and transform the dynamics you find yourself in, and to react quickly. Strength and speed and skills and tools, those are all very, very helpful, too. But if you can't evaluate and use what is appropriate in the moment, it doesn't matter how strong you are. It doesn't matter how big of a gun you carry or how sharp your knife is if in the moment you don't get it out and use it. If in the moment you are shell-shocked, then you are most likely going to perish. The way you do that is you fall back on old habits and patterns. Put those down, leave them where they lie, and allow the moment to show you, reveal to you, give to you what it has to offer and know that you can respond in the moment with all of your tools and skills at hand. That's your greatest gift.

Yes, you're bumbling around in the forest a bit but that doesn't mean you're a klutz and it doesn't mean you suck and it doesn't mean you don't have skills and talents. It simply means that right now your focus needs to be on what your feet are touching now, what your hands are touching now, what's happening right now. That's going to give you the opportunity to bring the completeness of you into this moment instead of trying to cram the old version of you into a new environment. If in your old environment you never had to worry about stepping on dried branches and in your new environment that's all you have to worry about, then you better get to the business of focusing on your new environment rather than reflecting on the skills that worked in your old environment. Do you understand?

Eighteen

We come to a village in our travels. Now, we know this village. This village has really good food, so we like this one. We stop here on our way wandering about, whatever we have to do, whenever we're in the neighborhood, just like you, you know where to get a good burrito, don't you? Well, in our day, that's not quite what we eat but a good soup with a nice mug of ale and a warm fire and if we have some women around that like to keep us company, we never turn that down either. So, there you go. This is what this village is. The village of good food. It has a name but we call it the village of good food.

The village of good food and good companionship and warm fires is where we are now. By this time, we will have fast-forwarded say five months or something, so 1, 2, 3, and 4 well, we're kind of getting used to having them around. We're not so sure about 4, but 1, 2, and 3 for sure. 4 has kind of got a little bit of an attitude. We might have to set that straight soon. So, we're in the village of good food and we're having a nice meal by a warm fire and it's nice to just let down a little bit. Let down a little bit. Everyone needs a little down-time, right?

So there we are, we are probably, what? How many are we now? Sixteen, it looks like, so we take up a considerable amount of the common room here at this place that we're stopping at for good food. We are not trying to make any statements. We are not trying to make any statements but like you, the truth of us is emanated. In your world, the truth of you being emanated doesn't always come across very viscerally. When we emanate the truth of us, it's kind of visceral. Especially when all sixteen of us are stuffed in one room and maybe we haven't bathed for a while. It's not our fault. We just got to the town of good food that also has baths. It's been a while. It's kind of cold outside. Do you want to bathe in that stream? Go right ahead. If you smell just as bad as the guy next to you, no one cares. So, we're sort of stinky, we admit it, and we're at the fire and getting stinkier and we're drinking and we're eating and we're enjoying the companionship of the ladies who wish to give us companionship, and some of the other men in the place aren't very comfortable with our emanations, whether it be odiferous or verbal or more importantly, the fact that we know how to handle ourselves, if you know what we mean.

The discomfort they feel is not our responsibility. Just like the discomfort people feel around you when you emanate the truth of you is not your responsibility. Now, not everyone feels uncomfortable around you when you emanate the truth of you, but certainly enough of them do that this is an appropriate topic. When you emanate the truth of you, when you have standards, when you stand up, when you demand conscious conversation, when you won't participate in unconscious conversation, this is you emanating the truth of you, right? Sometimes people have a little bit of a problem with it, right? So, in our example, we're not even bothering with that and we're already causing ruffled feathers over on the other side of the room. The thing is, we don't care what they think, but in your situations, a lot of times, the feathers that you ruffle are people that you actually care what they think—family members, bosses, coworkers—right?

What do you do when you ruffle the feathers of somebody and you care about their opinion? We recommend that you discontinue caring about their opinion. Why? Because you cannot change their opinion of you and if you discontinue emanating the truth of you, it would be like if all of a sudden we started being meek, started leaving our sharp bits behind and not bringing them with us everywhere we go. You can see how ridiculous that would be, yes? You discontinuing emanating the truth of you because it makes other people uncomfortable would be just as silly. You cannot say no to the truth of you because other people don't get it. You simply continue to say yes to the truth of you in order to facilitate the opportunity for growth that the truth of you presents. When you do this you may have to change your acquaintances. If they're family members, you may have to change your relationship to them. At some point, you put being the truth of you at the top of your list and then you fix things from there.

When you try to be the truth of you, and not be the truth of you based on who you're around, it looks a little something like this: Here we are in the pub, eating the food in the village of good food and five men walk in. Now, we decide for some reason we don't want those men to be uncomfortable in our presence, so everyone, all sixteen of us, simultaneously attempts to put all the sharp, pointy bits under the table. To strip off any sort of badges of honor or things that make us look tough and macho, as you would call it. So we're all taking things off and stuffing them under the table and pretending that we're not who we are. Ridiculous, yes, but this is what you do sometimes. People come into the room and you think, "Oh no, I cannot shine my light in front of them." You may not put that language on it but you know you do it and it's just as silly as us stuffing all of our things under the table.

This is why we tell you this story, because when we tell you this story you can see the things you do in a new light and the way you do this is by dimming your light, by changing your opinion about yourself. Now, you can imagine those first guys leave and another five men come in and we're not afraid to show our light in front of these guys. Maybe they're close friends. "Oh, it's OK for me to show my light in front of these people." Then we have to drag everything back out and put everything back on. Knives—strap them here and here and here and here and here. And oh God, 4, can't find his knife and he can't figure out what he's doing. We're going to have to get rid of him soon. We can just feel it. Put it all on again. And then it's like, "Hi! Nice to know you. Haven't seen you for a while. I know you so I can emanate the truth of me." Then those five people leave and another five come in and it all starts over again.

Now, we're telling you in this way because we want to show you what your body goes through energetically when you do this. Taking things off and putting things on physically, that's an example, a ridiculous example, but an example nonetheless, to point out what your body goes through when you shift from low vibration to high vibration, high vibration to low vibration. It's like taking off everything that identifies you and stuffing it some place out of sight. Why? Are you ashamed of it? Do you hide these things out of shame? Out of embarrassment? Out of fear? What makes you hide the truth of you? Eventually, it just becomes too much of a bother and/or impossible to fool around like that, so you stop. That's the invitation we offer you. When you are tempted to put down your light, to stop emanating the truth of you, to stop requiring conscious conversation, when you stop all those things, it is like us taking off our weapons simply because someone comes in the room that's uncomfortable with us. We hope that this fun little story in the village of good food will help you remember what it's like, what your body goes through.

Can you very well imagine us doing that every time? All sixteen of us. We're not small. Three has knocked over his tankard and 1 has his elbows in his food and 2 just stands there because he's kind of embarrassed about the whole thing. He doesn't know what to do. He's like, "Are we supposed to be putting or taking off at this point? I've lost track." They're a mess. We thought we were going to be happy about them after five months, but as it turns out, we're not as happy as we thought we were. We're going to have to do something about that. 4 is definitely gone. Are you attached to 4? Work it out. 4 is leaving the band, 4 has got to go.

Don't dim your light for anybody. If you have to dim your light, just remember how ridiculous it would look to see sixteen grown men try to get all their gear off and stuffed under the same damn table in a nano-second so as not to offend the sensibilities of the people who just happened to come into our place. When we started off this portion of our story, we thought, oh, this is a good example. Now that we are at the end of this section, we're disgusted with the damn story and we hope you never do anything silly like that so we never have to revisit the idea. Don't do that. Just don't do it. It would be so much easier on all of us. Now we're back to our tankards of ale. Another round for everyone!

Nineteen

In our story—1, 2, 3, and 4 are simply projections of the internal journey you're all experiencing—and old number 4, well, he's going to be something that is going to be released, laid down, and walked away from, gladly. Because one, he's noisy; two, he farts; three, he can't handle his beer. Exactly what good is he? All the bad things, and by bad we mean the things that suck—come on, let's be real. We don't have such compunction against the judgment idea. In our world if something doesn't work, you get rid of it. You know why? Because it could get you dead, and not just in this sort of pretend-ish way that you sometimes worry about getting dead. We mean by getting dead. Like literally stabbed. This noisy guy who smells bad—now, we know people think we stink. Fine. But he has the worst gas ever, ever experienced by anyone we know. How that happens we just don't even want to understand. And he gets drunk.

Now, we all enjoy having a beer or two or ten. No problem. But he gets drunk on like, one beer. And he doesn't stop. Guess what? He is what we call a liability. In you, liabilities are parts of you where you have yet to apply consciousness. Liabilities are places where you have yet to apply consciousness or places where you've applied consciousness and recognize that you're ready to lay it down and walk away from it. The liability for you is not so much that you're going to get dead or that you're going to have to smell his gas, but that you're going to experience yourself in a way that doesn't allow you to emanate your truth. You're going to be denying your truth because of these liabilities. That's why they're liabilities. They take you out of your truth. When you're ready to lay it down and walk away from it, you have to bring the truth of you to the moment in order to do so. This is important. When you're ready to lay it down and walk away from it, you don't lay it down and walk away from it from fear. You don't lay it down and walk away from it from anxiety or habit or last year's version of you. You lay it down and walk away from it from the most conscious place you're capable of assuming. From the most current and conscious place you're able to inhabit, you lay it down and walk away from it.

With old number 4, we just come into the truth of us and say, "Look, dude, you don't work with us well. You don't work with us well and we are going to move on and you are not welcome to come with us." His reaction to that statement is irrelevant to us. We've already made our choice. Just as when you lay it down and walk away from it, it's screaming and yelling and saying, "but I'm a good habit, but I've been with you 50 years habit, but I'm a person who's been in your life for 25 years, but we're related, but you're my employee," et cetera. Their noise should not deter you if you've made the decision from the most conscious and current version of you. When you've made the decision from a different version of you, it's very easy for their noise to deter you. Do you understand? This is why when you're really ready to lay something down and walk away, it is important to marshal your resources, to gather yourself, to become ready to ask for the highest, most current, and conscious version of you to attend to this.

By doing that, you empower yourself to have the experience of laying it down and walking away without regret or remorse and without attachment. When you're not quite sure and you're reacting from a place of you that's not the highest, most conscious, current version of you, you tend to just drag it along behind you. So if we say, "Number 4, you have to go," and he whines and complains and he says, "I'm not from here and you dragged me out into the woods and I'm at this nice inn but beyond that I don't know the land," and we start to feel sorry for him, and the next thing you know, we have him traipsing along behind us and we're still smelling his stinky gas and he's still making noise and he's probably still drunk. None of those things support us moving through the forest in a stealthy way, as you can well imagine. But your stinky, drunk and noisy habits tend to stay right along with you. You wrap them up in a sack and you drag them behind you, and they slow you down. Plus, they're drunk and they stink and they're noisy. You see why number 4 has to be so unpalatable? Because the truth of your habits are that they are equally unpalatable. It's only when you see them in such a light that you'll be liberated enough to allow the truth of you to attend to them, rather than the fears that you have to attend to them. Do you understand? So 4 has got to go. Because we are the narrator of this story, he goes peacefully. Most likely, he's going to end up staying in the town of good food and getting some kind of a job. Good. We'll send him off to be a blacksmith guy. He's big, so he can go make horseshoes. He'll be happy.

Shall we tell you about 3 a little bit? Number 3. Thing is, we kind of like number 3. Number 3 is kind of that guy—you call him the underdog. The guy who is never quite expected to win. He never is expected to win, so you root for him. We have sympathy for him. Because you see, we weren't always the way we are now. Just like you who were not always the way you are now, and many times you felt like an underdog, you felt like the cards were stacked against you, you felt like the chance of success was small, you felt like you had to climb and scrape and work very hard, and the challenges and the difficulties you faced along the way made it seem like there was very little chance of winning, right?

So we look at number 3 and he's kind of that guy. He's that guy that gets it on the last try. He's that guy that kind of screws up on a regular basis but always kind of comes through just at the end. He reminds us of that part of ourselves that we had to work on very diligently and he reminds us to be kind to that part of ourselves that is still growing, that's still transforming. We're keeping 3 around. You know why? Because there are parts of us that we still have that same underdog feeling about; and there are parts of you that you still have that same underdog feeling about. There is still that part of you that you think, "Am I ever going to be past this challenge?"

For example, 3 was off trying to set up a shelter. Do they not have rain where he comes from? Has he never had to make a shelter before? You just wonder. Eric, did you never show him how to make something that would keep the rain off, or did you just let him sit in the rain, literally? It's a good thing Eric is gone. We are more and more disappointed in Eric's leadership skills as the days go by. So, here is number 3. He doesn't even know how to properly put together a shelter for himself. The men have sort of taken him under their wing a little and they've showed him and they've showed him and sure enough, his shelter has fallen on him again and it's the middle of the night and he's drenched wet out there trying to fix his shelter.

Now, some of you might think he's going to go the way of 4 really soon.

And you know why he won't? Because he never stops trying. So we will go out of our shelter and help him right now. Just like that part where you have uncovered the layer of the onion after the layer of the onion after the layer of the onion—you will go to that part of you again and you will attend to the next layer of the onion that has been discovered. You will get wet together but you'll build a shelter and you'll transform the situation and you may feel soggy afterward, and you may feel like it was almost too hard, but you'll keep going. You'll keep trying, you'll keep attending, you'll keep, keep, keep transforming. You may feel like the underdog in that way, but who doesn't love an underdog?

So when you find yourself feeling like the underdog, remember our story and remember the fact that number 3, even though his shelter keeps falling on him, he's appreciated because he doesn't give up. Appreciate yourself for the fact that you don't give up.

Twenty

We left the village of good food. We left number 4 behind. He became a blacksmith. And that life suited him well. He was a big boy, after all, so there you go. Number 3, well, we have a soft spot for number 3 so he's pretty solid now.

When we went to see the king, a while ago, we told you that one of the things that we do when we go to see the king is we take a look around, get the lay of the land on a number of levels. One level is we look around for people we might want to bring into our band. There was one we had our eye on back when we went to see the king last time. Now let's say it's been eight or nine months, so we want to go back to the castle.

They're lots of good things that happen at the castle. We've shared these before. We like the company at the castle. We like the food at the castle. And the castle gives you some opportunities to buy new pointy sharp things, to get kind of the scoop about what's going on. You do this by going on the Internet, primarily, these days. Maybe you read the newspaper; maybe you go down to the local coffee shop, whatever you like to do. Every once in a while, it feels good to touch in and see what's going on with everybody else, so you know what this feeling is. One of the reasons we want to go into the castle is because we want to see about this young boy. Part of what happens with us is that there are jobs that none of us want to do. To be frank. We're not especially fond of certain jobs, so it's good to have a boy or two around. If we found a girl that we thought wanted to do this job, well we'd have her, too, but the thing is, in this time that we are in, girls don't have these kinds of jobs.

We need a boy or two around to help us out with things and there often tends to be spare boys around. This is a very tough time to live. People die. It's a fact of life. People are dying all the time and there are spare kids around. It's just a fact. So there's this boy, Cedric, we had our eye on when we were last at the castle and we liked him because he had a very inquisitive mind, he was very aware, and he was quiet. If they're quiet at the castle, chances are they're quiet in the forest, and we kind of like the quiet ones. See number 4 if you wonder about that.

We're going to go look him up. Plus, this guy over here—he doesn't want you to know his name, he's a little undercover that way—he needs a few medical things taken care of. So we need to go to the castle. Now, the interesting thing is as we come out of the forest, people get a little bit attentive to our presence. Just like when you're emanating the truth of you, people are attentive to your presence in a different way. Right? See, there's a moral to this story. We come out of the forest and it can feel to people as if we appeared out of nowhere. We like this quite a lot.

Part of what happens is that when we show up people make associations. A lot of time they think, "Oh, something bad must be happening if these guys are in town." That's a little bit of the unfortunate aspect of having a reputation. Oh, well. We're looking for Cedric while we are walking up and, sure enough, because Cedric is a bright boy who pays attention, there he is. We like him a lot because the first thing he does is offer us information. When you have something to offer, you're very attractive to other people. Now, is Cedric being of service? No. Cedric is emanating his truth, which is: "I'm very good at accumulating information and disseminating it in ways that help me." He has some information for us and he's polite. Quiet and polite and inquisitive. You see why we've had our eye on this one for a while. He comes up and he says, "You know, some of the king's men are not exactly being polite to the king." This is interesting information, indeed. Because the king's men are supposed to be sworn to loyalty and all that, right? Well, we saw from Eric's boys how that goes. The king's men are supposed to be loyal to the king and Cedric says that he's been hearing some grumbling. This concerns us because, you know, we like this king.

Off we go into the castle. Cedric, of course, has already scored us a place to stay and everything is going pretty well and Cedric says, "You know, I'm worried. I'm worried because I hear the grumbling of the men who work for the king." Of course, you know what that means. We have to go see the king again. And damn it, we didn't roll around in the mud or anything. So, opportunity missed. Anyway, Cedric is not just a stable boy for the king as much as he's just sort of everywhere at once, so he can get us kind of close to the guy who can get us to see the king, and the king knows us so it's not as though we have to wait and wait for a formal introduction. We roll into town and say, "Yo, we need to talk to you." The king is going to listen if the king is in the mindset to listen. Unfortunately, the king is not in the mindset to listen at this time and now we know why his men are grumbling.

The king is distracted by a woman. Now, we love women, don't get us wrong. We love women a lot. But this is the kind of woman that you just don't want your king distracted by. She's come for a visit from some neighboring kingdom, it's all king business—you know how much we like that—and when she comes to town, part of what happens is the king stops thinking about king business and starts thinking about King Business, if you know what we mean. This is the kind of woman who is not in it to benefit the people. She's in it to benefit herself and the king is a little en-chanted by her. This is why the men are not happy because the men are feeling like the king is not attending to business. Being distracted from the moment, being distracted from your growth, we'll just call her Ms. Habit. She represents habit in our story. The habit to, how shall we say, focus on things that are not what is in your lap.

The king's men are concerned because things aren't being attended to as far as defense of the kingdom, as far as attention to some of the neigh-bors, let's say, that often need to be looked after, et cetera. And Cedric is concerned because, well, Cedric is one of these kids that would probably be on the front line if something happens, so he's a little worried about sticking around the old castle. He is starting to want to come along with us and we're having a little side conversation with him about that because we are starting to want him to come along with us too. So, that's good for us. Time passes a bit and we're still at the castle and we still haven't seen the king and that's starting to be not OK because, after all, we have something important to say. We use some of our abilities, let's just call it, to get into the king's room. If you ever want to see a shocked look on a king's face, show up in his bedchambers without him knowing how you got there. It helps to have some skills of which he's not aware. This called for showing a hand or two. Cedric is good at getting us in places, as well.

So, we look at the king and we say, "Hey, we hear there are some problems." And he's like, "What? There are no problems here." Yeah. "I am not going to look at the moment. I am going to remember the embrace of the lovely Ms. Habit rather than attend to what's real and in front of me." We say, "Well, we got into your chambers." "Oh, but you're who you are." "Yes, but what if we were here to kill you? What if we were sent here and we decided to take the job to kill you?" "But you wouldn't." "But what if? Let's be real. You're not paying attention to what is in your lap. You're busy trying to get something else in your lap, if you know what we mean. The relationship you have with this woman is not supporting your growth."

You see, this is what happens is you get into relationships that stop supporting your growth and your movement forward spiritually and instead they distract you and bring you into habit. You let it go on. Just like the king is letting it go on. He's letting this woman play this role in his life. We could have given him a man. We're just picking a woman for fun. Stereotypes. Stories include stereotypes. He says, "Oh, but you haven't met her." And we say, "And we don't want to. We have no interest. If she and your choices around her are causing you to ignore your kingdom in this way, we have no interest in her." Why? Because we only associate with people who raise our vibration, who help us become more of ourselves, who help us emanate our truth more. "A true queen will support the kingdom first, not her own wishes. She would not distract you from that which is your calling; which is to rule." He says, "Oh, but you haven't met her."

We think, "Oh, we're in trouble now." We have to get the hell out of here because he's repeating himself and he's not listening and this is not the king we know. Since we've liked this man before…hmm…we may have to put our hands on the king. We know he could have us murdered for this, but none of his men will listen to him anyway at this point. When you grab someone by the front, it's really, really great if you can lift him off his feet at the same time. If you're that strong, we advise doing that because it really gets his attention when you can lift him off his feet. Old Cedric. We know he's peeking through the hole in the wall. We know his eyes are *this big*. "Oh my God, you're manhandling the king." He's thinking, "What's the fastest way out of the castle?" Because he's afraid now.

When you grab the king you're really putting it on the line. This is when you're saying, "My truth is more important than anything else." You grab the king and you lift him off his feet and you get real close to him and you know you had garlic for dinner, so it's real good, you're nice and stinky which really gets his attention and you say "What is your truth? Who are you and what is the truth you are emanating? Because the truth that you're showing is not the man we know. The truth that you're showing right now is not the man the rest of your people know either and they're afraid. And that's 100 percent on you." Just as it's 100 percent on you to emanate your truth and decide: Are you going to be distracted by habit or are you going to allow the relationships you create to support the truth of you being emanated in this world? We want the king to have a queen. Absolutely, of course we do. But we want the king to choose a queen who supports and helps him grow just as he supports and helps her grow, which in turn helps the kingdom grow. Not one that distracts him and keeps him from his business.

Now, when you go to set someone down that you've picked up by the front of their clothing, it's especially nice if there's something behind them that you can push them onto. It helps with the whole thing you're doing. Luckily, since we're in his bedchamber, we can push him onto his bed. Now, the king hasn't been manhandled since he was a boy. That gets his attention. Shakes him out of it enough. Breaks the habit. It's a big risk but we're willing to take it. And then what do we do? We turn and leave. Why? Because the choice to emanate the truth of you is a decision that requires free will and cannot be usurped by anyone else and he must make the choice on his own. We've done our part. We walk out of the chamber. We look at Cedric and we say, "Are you ready to be with us?" And he says, "Absolutely. Let's get the hell out of here," and away we go.

Twenty-one

We grabbed the king and shook him a little because he has that woman. He's been distracted by a woman, and it's all well and beautiful to be distracted by a fine woman—we have been many times and we will be many times again—but to be distracted by a woman who does not have your best interests at heart and, of course, if you're a ruler and she does not have that best interest of your kingdom at heart, well, that's just foolish. The king is being foolish. A man who can have just about any woman in the kingdom and chooses that—he needed to be shook around a little to see if it rattles his brain a bit. But, on the other hand, he is the king, so it's probably a good idea for him to see the backside of us real soon. Cedric wants to come with us and we consider the whole thing a success because Cedric is now going to be with us.

Now, we told the story of Eric and we told you how Eric fit in, and we want to tell you right now how Cedric fits in. Cedric is representative of the part of you that you're still learning to love. The part of you that is still growing on you. The part of you that still doesn't have everything coordinated. The part of you that is the inner child. The part of you that has a lot of potential but hasn't quite grown into it. We're just giving you a clue of how Cedric fits into the story. So, as we take Cedric along we see ourselves there. We see ourselves there as a young man. Now, Cedric isn't small. He's young but he's not small, or else we wouldn't be interested in him. He's quite big already. But he's gangly, as you would say, and he's a little bit confused by the shifting roles that he finds himself in. Because he found himself first as this sort of observer in the kingdom, and then he found himself as a confidant of ours, and now he finds himself afraid that the king is going to be angry and come after us. But he also finds himself attracted to leaving the castle and going with us. It's something he's always wished to do. Does this sound sort of like your inner world? "I'm four things at once and none of them feel good."

As Cedric runs alongside us he is looking for guidance, and these parts of yourself that you're confused about look to you for guidance, as well. This is where the spiritual discipline comes in. The discipline to love the parts of you that are not yet graceful; the discipline to love the parts of you that are confused. To love the parts of you that are aimless. To love the parts of you that are immature. To love them enough to help them along rather than to stuff them, or ignore them, or allow your fear of them to put them out of your mind. When you personalize it and you make it Cedric, it's easy to see that you wouldn't just put Cedric out of your mind after you asked him to come along with you. That would be stupid. But there is an energetic inside of you that tempts you to push aside, to ignore your unhealed aspects, and there's no way for them to heal and transform unless you bring them into the light of day. Just as there's no way for Cedric to grow up as a strong man unless he has some guidance. You can see that correlation, right? So, on with the story. We've done the meta-physical bit. Now, let's see what kind of mischief we can get into.

So as we're running down this hallway, and you can picture it with the torches in the wall made of stone, and we're running along and Cedric's kind of scared and we're laughing because we think it's funny that we just pushed the king onto his bed. The guards are clattering around and they're sort of unhappy with the king anyway, so they're not all that excited about having to do anything for him right now. The king has been on a downhill slope for a while now, so everyone's a little pissed off. But they're loyal, so they're going to do what the king says. So, they're clattering up to see what's going on with the king and we're just wondering what that old king is going to do. Is old king-y going to try to send his ridiculous troops after us? That would be stupid because he's going to need us next week or next month, and if he sends all these clattery people after us we're not going to be as inclined to come back and say hi to him again. The king knows he's being an idiot. He just needed to be told by someone he respects. Now, is the king going to go unconscious and bury that and use this anger in order to get his way and show that he's the king? Or is the king going to call his advisers and say, "OK, seriously, have I been that much of an idiot? Is it really like that?" Well, we'll see what king-y does later but we're running down the hallway for now.

We're running down the hallway with Cedric. He knows all the ins and outs of the castle, which is awesome because then we don't have to go past all the clattery guards. They do make an awful lot of noise. We get down and we go this way and that way and in and out and round and about, and we get out to the stables. Cedric is freaking out at this point because he realizes, "Oh my God, I am going to change my whole life right now." And this is where you have been. "I'm going to make the choice. I'm going to make the choice to create my reality rather than be a victim of my circumstances. Am I going to stay here and be a stable boy because that's what I was born into, or am I going to create my reality by walking out of this castle with this band of warriors? What choice am I going to make?" Again it's very clear when you see it from Cedric's eyes that he's either creating his reality or choosing to be a victim. Be like Cedric. Be courageous. Cedric's scared shitless but he's going with us anyway.

We get going on the horses and he says, "Well, what about, what about…" and we say, "Oh no, Cedric, you have to understand. We don't go into the king's chambers and bully him without letting everybody know. Everybody knows just exactly what we intended to do and they are already in the forest waiting for us." Cedric realizes—the dawning of the light of consciousness—that he is part of a community now. A community that keeps each other informed and a community that supports each other's growth, supports each other's plans, supports each other's ideas. A community that believes in the idea of sticking together and teaming up and showing respect. Cedric thinks, "You mean, all of your men knew you were going into the king's chamber with the intent to rough him up, and they didn't run and panic, they are waiting for us? They're not afraid, they're not hiding, they're waiting for us?" And old Cedric thinks, "Wow, if I could be in an environment where I could trust like that, if I could believe like that…" it starts to get real attractive. It helps him to believe that he will be cared for and loved and supported in a way that even crazy ideas, seemingly crazy ideas, can be aired out. That it can be OK to say, "I feel afraid or nervous or confused" out loud and be honest about the truth of him and emanate the truth of him. "If the leader can do something as insane as sneaking into the king's chambers and roughing him up, then almost nothing I could come up with would be anywhere near that crazy, so maybe it is safe enough to be the complete truth of me in his presence." Do you see how this works?

Off we go into the forest. It's very quiet. And old Cedric, you know what? He's quiet, too, so we like him even more. We've liked him from the beginning but the fact that he's quiet seals the deal for us. It's nice because he'll take care of the horses in a very good way. He's quite good with the beasts and that's going to come in handy because we use horses quite a lot in what we do. Sometimes we walk around, but if we have horses we're happy about it, and right now we have horses. As it turns out one of the men who was enjoying the company of a fine woman and having a bath and some good food found out about something. He found out about something down the way and over the hill and across a river or two that we want to look into. And we're going to take old Cedric with us. Because, you know what happens? The parts of us that need to be developed, the parts of us that need to be transformed, the parts of us that are those shadow places, you know where we put them? On the horse right in front of us so we can keep a good eye on them and make sure anything they need, want, or desire that we are capable of offering, we offer. Why? Because we want healing above all else, and in wanting healing above all else we keep a real keen eye on the aspects that need transformation. Old Cedric is what needs transformation and he's giving his all. So we, in turn, give our all to him and together we grow. You grow as you give your all to attending to the places within you that need attention.

Twenty-two

Off we go. Cedric is with us and he's great because he takes care of the horses, he doesn't complain, and he's not noisy. Over the hill and down the woods, or whatever you say in your fairytales, we hear there is a beastie who is marauding. How often do you get to say the word "marauding"? Now, "beastie" is a catchall phrase for anything that isn't a human. We have no idea what the beastie is and the great thing about the time we live in is that there is no Internet, there are no telephones, and there is no way, really, to get information from one end of the kingdom to the other except by passing it with couriers or by gossip or word-of-mouth. The longer it takes for the story to reach us, the wilder the story becomes. We have been called on to take care of a dragon breathing fire which turned out to simply be a boar.

When we hear stories about marauding beasties, on some level we think: Oh boy, this could be tough. On another level we think: It could just be another one of those little rumors. This is what we want to invite you to do. When you experience something, don't have a preconceived notion of it. Don't decide ahead of time what is actually happening. Allow yourself to be aware in the moment of what is happening. You have to trust yourself to attend to whatever shows up in order to pull this off. It saves you from being afraid that you're going to face a dragon the whole time when it turns out that you will be facing a wild boar. You see? Did you follow that? Do we need to say it again?

Otherwise, you fret that it's going to be a big fire-breathing dragon instead of allowing that when you show up you'll attend to whatever's there. That's important. Because you spend a lot of time projecting what the future's going to hold instead of experiencing the reality that you're in. And right now, the reality is, we're riding a horse, Cedric's in front of us, and we're getting ready to have some food. That's the reality we're in. When we get to the village that is not that far away, when we get there we will attend to what's there and the beauty of this is thus. We know we will have all our tools with us, we will show up prepared, and we will be in the moment with whatever we find. Sound like something you'd like to do? Fretting about it right now only makes this journey through the forest suffering. Yes?

We're walking through the forest, we're going to have some lunch, Cedric is going to look after the horses, we're going to teach him how to throw knives because that's a fun thing to do after you've eaten. Before you get back on your horse, you teach Cedric how to throw knives. Maybe tomorrow we'll teach him how to shoot a bow and arrow. Would we want to miss that by fretting about the dragon? Cedric is not quite aware that this is how you handle it. So, Cedric says, "Sir, what about the dragon? What about the dragon?" And we say: Cedric you need to go find that knife, you just missed the tree. "Yes, sir, but I was so busy thinking about the dragon." Yes we know. That's why you need to go find the knife. You missed the tree because you were thinking about the dragon. When there's a dragon in front of you, you're going to want to be able to hit it, so you best practice right now with the tree. You get it?

Cedric keeps throwing the knife and we know that the idea that he can attend to this moment hasn't exactly calmed him. Because when he's throwing the knife he feels like, "Oh God, I have to get it right because it'll be a dragon soon." That's what you do, as well. You fear that when you need your tools you won't quite know how to use them. Therefore, when you're practicing you distract yourself and you make it more difficult to actually hit your mark. Again, the moment, the moment, the moment. Because we know that 99.9 percent of the time when they call us for a beastie, it's not a dragon. It's really something that we're going to have for dinner.

You don't eat dragon. Did you know that? Dragon is poisonous. You don't eat dragon. Just checking. Don't let the dogs eat it either because it's not good for dogs even. Nobody eats the dragon. It's best to bury them whole.

We know, as you hopefully have become aware, that most of the time—and by most we mean like 95 percent of the time—the thing that you have built up to be afraid of turns out to be much more mundane. It's very, very rarely a flying, fire-breathing dragon; it's much more often something like a wild boar that's digging up the potatoes. Because you're addicted to drama when you're in an unconscious position and because the survival instinct is so powerful in you and it has to look for danger at all times, your body wants to believe it's going to be the dragon and it tells you it's going to be the dragon because it thinks that prepares you. The reality is when you override that and you stay in the moment, you're actually preparing in real-time rather than pseudo-preparing, which is basically just running adrenaline and fear in you. Got it?

Throw the knife into the tree and that in-the-moment practice and application of your tools will allow you to be ready when and if an opportunity comes where you need to use that tool.

Twenty-three

They've called us in to deal with the beastie. This beastie turns out to be near the place of nice hot water. This is especially good because it's getting kind of wintry and it takes a while to get to this place, maybe a month or so. This is the place of the good hot water and by that, of course, we mean these hot springs. You have them, so you know what we're talking about. There's just a place here in the forest where you go and you get naked and you get in the hot springs. Now, as we've pointed out, we don't mind smelling bad but we sure do like warm water when it's offered. So we go to the place of the good hot water and nearby they have a beastie problem. Our suspicion is it's something like a wild boar but as we get closer and closer, the stories gets wilder and wilder. We know why they've called for us; they're scared shitless. Now there are always, always, always—we'll tell you some things about when they call you to deal with the beasties—there are always missing children, there are always missing animals, and there are always indecipherable tracks in the mud. Guaranteed, you're going to have those three stories.

It's not always that the dragon or whatever has made off with the children. Sometimes the children have been made off with by other means. And the animals? Well, animals come and go in this world. The indecipherable tracks? There's a lot of mud in our world. Anything close to where the town is? Good luck tracking anything. It's a mess. We're good at it but it's still a mess. None of those stories ever get our attention very strongly, but this one has the story of the strange sounds. They don't always have stories of strange sounds because most people around here know the sounds the nearby animals make. You probably would be concerned if you heard certain animals outside your door because you're not used to hearing certain animals outside the door. Your dogs, your cats, your birds, whatever, you are used to those. But if all a sudden a bear was outside or a wolf or a coyote or even a fox, you would be on alert. These people know all those sounds. None of those sounds surprise them. They're used to it. A bear comes ambling by, "Well, thank God we had the door shut." They're not as freaked out about things like that. But there are strange sounds happening. The strange sounds get our attention because then maybe it's going to be something new. Yeah!

As we're sitting in the hot water, we hear the strange sound! You can just imagine all of us getting out of the hot water simultaneously, buck naked, looking for our sharp pointy things that are nearby, swinging, as you might imagine the visual—we know you appreciate it, it's pretty funny. So, as we're swinging, looking around for what's making the sound, we're thinking, "Wow, something new is in the forest." And of course, if something new is in the forest for us what does that mean? Something new is inside you, right? Something new is inside you and it's coming forward to be seen. It's coming forward to be seen.

Now, just like we don't know what kind of beastie this is, you don't necessarily know what you're bringing forward. You're aware that it's some sort of beastie that you've wrestled with in the past, but if you knew all about it you would know its nature. You wouldn't have it hidden in you. You would've already dealt with it if you were clear on how to go about it. If you knew how to handle that thing that you've been dragging around with you, that's been lurking inside of you, that's been hiding, if you knew just what to do, you would have attended to it already. But it's this thing, it's another layer of the onion and it's going around and around and it's coming forward and you're like, "I know I have an issue around x, y, z, but it's stuck to me." Just as this beastie is stuck in the forest and it doesn't come clearly from behind the trees where we can get a look at it, to see what sort of sharp pointy thing might be good to have ready to use, and to know whether or not we have time to put on some more clothing. It is winter, after all, so you can imagine the visual, right?

As we hear this sound and as we imagine what kind of beastie goes with that noise, we just listen, and that's what we ask you to do, is to listen to what is true in you. Listen to what your heart says to you. Listen to what it is you desire in your life. Listen and know what it is. Listen closely. Take that time. Take that moment. Even if triggered, and we are triggered right now, the adrenaline is pumping, the beastie could come out of the forest at any moment and we're ready—sort of, if you count not having any clothes on as being ready. Sometimes you feel like that, too. Naked, exposed, confused, disoriented, not grounded and settled. And what do you do? You still have to deal with the beastie even if you don't feel all ready and prepared and meditated.

What do you do? How do you attend to the beastie that comes out when you're not prepared? What you remember is what you have learned. What you remember is that you have a foundation. Maybe you feel a little out of sorts in the moment but you have a foundation under your feet. We know we can swing this sword. We know that this one over here is really good with the bow and arrow. We know this one over there has a cross bow out. There is a foundation under us. We may be in the moment a little out of sorts, naked and all, but we have a foundation that comes with us even if we're out of sorts. Even if we're out of sorts, there's a foundation there. Even when you feel a bit out of sorts, there's still a foundation under you. There's still something to fall back on. There's still something to give of yourself even if you don't have 100 percent of you working. "I don't feel rested. I don't feel fed. I don't feel this. I don't feel that." There is still something there that is more than before, when you had no training.

Out of the forest this big beastie comes. We estimate it's about five feet tall as it comes bounding out of the forest toward us. It turns out that the sound it makes is the sound of joy. It's so slobbery, you have no idea. But the damn thing comes bounding up and instead of barking or jumping or attacking or any of those things, it does that thing dogs do where it puts its butt up in the air and it puts its arms out in the front and it yips. It's ridiculous. You have no idea how ridiculous this is. We're looking at this thing and we think: Oh hell, we're going to have to take the thing with us. Why? You can't kill a big, three-headed puppy thing. We can't kill the thing. But these people are going to end up killing it because it's just too much for them. But you know what? No trigger is too much for us. Why? Because, like you, we want healing above all else. Even if it is a three-headed, 5-foot-tall, yippy, slobbering, needing-to-be-fed thing. We kind of like the unusual and we're not afraid to look at what comes out of the forest at us. We figure in all our travels we haven't met anybody who'd befriend a three-headed slobbering pup. Nobody, right? So, what would you think if we left him behind? No way.

So it's going to fall to Cedric— we knew it was a good idea to bring that guy along. Cedric is good with the beasties, as we've previously explained, and Cedric likes the name Riley for the dog.

Cedric and Riley. Now, if you have a 5-foot-tall, three-headed dog, you know what you can do? You can ride him. If you're Cedric. Guess what Cedric wants to do? Cedric wants to teach Riley to be his horse.

What did we tell you that Cedric represents? Cedric represents the parts of us that desire transformation. Riley is the unknown coming forward. So, Riley represents a trigger; that part of us that we haven't identified. Cedric represents that which we've already identified. Riley represents that part of us that we're still trying to pull out and get into full focus—and they got together and they're causing mischief. Soon, we will leave the town of good hot water and we will move on to some other place with Riley getting used to Cedric riding him. We like old Riley already. Why? Because we like to set our shit out where we can have a good gander at it.

Twenty-four

We're going to take this beastie away from this village and we need to get a move on because while Cedric is all fond of it already of course not everybody else is. That's the energetic where it's all well and good to have a beastie that you like, but you don't necessarily want him to be quite close to the village where the village people might decide they're not happy having a three-headed dog stick around. So, although that village was pleasant to be in and will forever be known as the village where we got Riley, we're going to get a move on. We have decided to continue moving eastward. We'll tell you, we started off this story with just our guys, and then we picked up some of Eric's guys, and then we got Cedric, and now we have Riley; and it's starting to feel a little bit motley, if you understand what we mean. It's a bit like, what the hell has happened? We've gathered a lot of things and we're not quite sure how they all fit together. Sound familiar?

Here you have all these different tools and aspects of yourself and uncovered parts of you and places in you that are new to you, and places in you that you've healed and transformed and you're still a little bit uncertain about. It's all well and good to have a three-headed dog with you, but how exactly does it fit in? There's a lot of how-exactly-does-it-fit-in energy that we feel from you. "How exactly does it fit in to walk around with the truth of me? How exactly does it fit in to walk around in clarity? How exactly does it all fit together?" The truth of the matter is it fits together as you decide that each piece has a value of its own and that it fits together as you walk it, as you move through, as you go. As we walk through the forest, we feel our way into how they all go together. We see that number 2 likes the three-headed dog as well. Cedric is quite fond of this gentleman over to our right who is extremely deadly with the bow and arrow, which is good because we really want Cedric to be quite skilled, so it's good that he has friends here that are teaching him how to use the bows and arrows and all that kind of stuff that's so important. Just as you learn, you find, you reso-nate with different teachers or other books, or you look at a tree and it tells you something new. You start to make a completeness of you. The beauty of this is it's never finished, so don't seek for it to be done. You always add more. There's always something more. There's always a new skill. There's always a new handhold. There's always a new grip.

As we move along through the forest, one of the things that we're doing as we travel slowly—we're not in a hurry, we're just taking our time and enjoying ourselves—is integration. Part of what's going on with our band is we need to integrate and find each other's balance again. Just as you are doing. You're integrating and coming into a deeper balance. Integration and balance are the next steps on the journey to ascension, the journey to Homo spiritus. Becoming more balanced in all of your chakras. Becoming more balanced in your ability to process, perceive, experience triggers in a new way. Becoming more balanced in your experience of habit. Becoming more balanced in the integration of your alternative expressions. Becoming more balanced. There is a peacefulness to a balanced state that you will really enjoy. Walking through the forest from a balanced position allows you to handle the potential fears, to handle the beauty, to handle the men, to handle the experiences you have in a new way, bringing forth the truth of you and holding it at all times as your greatest and most prized posses-sion. The truth of you is the most important thing for you to be conscious of, understand, experience, revel in. "What is true about me? What is the truth of me? What is the greatest gift I can give myself? What is the most loving act I can do right now for me?" All of these things are so preciously important.

In times in between the more thrilling bits of our story, we are integrating, balancing, seeing how the men work together. That's how you function: You integrate, you balance, you see how the new aspects of you work together. The uncovered dark spots. The uncovered shadow spots. When those things are uncovered and revealed and worked with, how then do you integrate that knowledge, that wisdom, that awareness, into your day-to-day life? When you become aware of something you've stuffed or hidden, how do you integrate that into your day-to-day life? How do you make peace with it? That's really an important aspect; it's not thrilling and exciting to be walking through the forest looking at the men, but it's important anyway. There's so much thrilling and exciting that goes on in your life, it's OK when you're at a period where there's a little bit of a lull to allow yourself integration time. It's just as important. Allow yourself these moments of integration, of awareness. Integration and awareness are very, very important.

Twenty-five

Cedric is learning to ride Riley. You have to remember Cedric is small in that way that you know he's going to be huge, but he's not huge yet. He's young. He's only like 12 or 13. Twelve or thirteen is a much more mature 12- or 13-year-old than what you have these days, of course. If you have no parents and you're running around a stable just trying to stay alive, you grow up pretty fast. But his body hasn't gotten there yet. The benefit of that is he gets to ride a three-headed dog, so every once in a while there's something to be said for staying the size you are for a little while.

Riley and Cedric, ugh, you have no idea. A big 5-foot-at-the-shoulder three-headed dog eats an enormous amount of food. The thing is, we don't have any idea how this beastie stayed alive because it doesn't seem to be very good at securing its own food supply. You'd think that is absolutely impossible. It has three mouths, after all. But it has three brains and it seems to have some confusion about stalking and catching and this eye over here is looking this way and this eye over here is looking that way and the middle one is sort of like, "Come on guys, let's get it together." It's a mess. This beastie is the most confused, strange, slobbering... at least it's not that noisy. It can move through the forest in a quiet way, but you have no idea how much food it eats. Every once in a while you have an animal that snores, right? Three heads, do we need to say any more? It eats, its snores, it barks, it slobbers times three, and it's 5 feet tall. It only has one asshole. There's a lot of shitting that goes on. If you had to shit for three mouths you'd be pretty busy, too.

You should just see it. Cedric gets on Riley and the outside heads are trying to look around and say, "What are you doing?" The middle one is going, "I can't see!" It's just a wreck. We just hope they're going to be quiet and they are sometimes. Thank goodness we're not trying to be too stealthy at this point.

Riley's three heads are funny and they illuminate the idea of the conflict between the parts of you that you're trying to learn about and your brain that would rather think ten other thoughts than the one you're trying to focus on. Cedric is trying to focus on teaching Riley to be his mount and Riley has three heads and they're all thinking different thoughts pretty much simultaneously. This is a little bit like what it is inside your head. You're always thinking different thoughts and many times they are just distractions from what is really going on. What's really going on, of course, is the revelation of the internal journey you're experiencing and how it is keeping you in suffering and fear and not letting you out into the conscious journey. The conscious journey here, of course, being carrying Cedric through the forest and getting to the next kingdom and the rest of it being whatever else this beastie tends to think about.

The good thing about this beastie is he's extraordinarily loyal and he's already worked out that he wants to be with us and we know the next time we get into a scrape, just imagine. We like to show up with pointy things all the time. You show up with a three-headed, 5-foot-tall dog, people are not going to fuck with you. We just know it. This is guaranteed to cut down the number of times we have to stab people. Which, in our line of work, is a considerable benefit.

Twenty-six

Turns out that there is another king that needs our help. You have to understand there's no Internet and there are no cell phones, so by the time the king's men find us tromping along in the forest and Riley barks at them and Cedric says, "Come here, Riley!" and Riley slobbers and everybody has their pointy things out and they say, "Go see the king because the king needs your help," well, it takes us a little while to get there because we don't exactly rush. Why exactly would we rush? We're kind of in the moment, so we figure whatever's going on it's going to be going on for a while.

We roll in and do our thing; and we're all ready to be muddy and dirty and stinky because that's our favorite way to greet kings, and oh shit, it's a queen and she's beautiful and her name's Marianna. And, oh God, shit, we could've taken a bath but we didn't know it was a queen and all the men are looking at us and she's looking at us and we're thinking "Oh, boy, we didn't see this coming. Didn't see this coming. Here's a big change. Didn't see this big change coming. Wow, we're not exactly putting our best foot forward," which is a very uncomfortable position for us to be in because we always put our best foot forward, especially when we go see the king, because we always show up stinky. What happens this time? We show up and we're stinky and we know we're not putting our best foot forward. And we think, "Oh, new experience." Without her even saying a word we are already feeling unsettled. This is the power a woman can have over a man. We would challenge any man that we've ever encountered or expect to encounter to any kind of a pointy instrument duel that he is interested in having, and we would feel completely settled. We walk stinky into the presence of this woman and the next thing you know, we're quivering a little bit. We don't quiver. This is uncomfortable. This is not good. This is the first sign that something big is changing for us and it's not easy for us to consider, as you can well imagine.

Then she goes ahead and gets up off her pretty chair and walks over to us and is there and she smells nice and she's got pretty skin and her hands.... And the men are thinking, "What the hell? This is bad." Because they've never seen us flustered. So we kind of take a deep breath and swallow and say, "At your service, your Majesty." Because we don't know what else to say. It's awkward as hell and the men have now begun to guffaw. If there's anything more embarrassing than being struck wobbly knees in front of the queen, it's when your men guffaw. Our men have never guffawed at us while sober, ever, so this is bad and getting worse by the second, because we don't know how to have a heart chakra. Maybe you can resonate with that. Oh, crap—all of a sudden, there it is.

So, she says something beautiful like, "Would you please have tea with me?" or something like that and we're completely enamored and we say the words, "May we bathe first?" We actually said it. May we bathe before we have tea? Here we are—we can be stinky and drop mud and do what we normally do, and clink and clank and the men can sneak around and get into all the positions to make sure our backs are covered, and what do we say? May we bathe first? So, here we are thinking we can't smell when we have tea. It's a big change. You see how difficult it is to make that change. How difficult it is to take the confidence you have in one way of being and infuse that truth into a way of being that's completely uncertain, insecure, and confusing. This is why we tell this story.

You've seen us do all kinds of things. We threw the other king down. We're not afraid of the nobility or any of that stuff. We're not afraid if they say, "Oh, we think there's a beastie in the forest." We were not afraid when Eric's men wanted to fight with us. We're not afraid of any of that. Why? Because those are our strongest chakras and we are very confident in operating from them. We have our feet under our shoulders when we come from the third chakra. Or the third eye. Even the root chakra—our home is wherever we go. But that damn fourth chakra gets kicked in and boy howdy, you'd think we were 16 again. Old Cedric might have a better shot at this than we do. Why? Because although we have an incredible amount of skill, we do not have a complete sense of balance—and neither do you.

Our story illuminates what it looks like, in kind of a humorous and em-barrassing way, what it's like when you're not balanced. Now is the time to become more comfortable in the chakras that you haven't felt comfortable working with. If it's your heart chakra or your root chakra or your power chakra or your throat chakra, whichever one you just don't know what to do with, well, you're in good company. Because here we are asking for a bath when we could burp and fart a little and make the queen nervous and upset and confused.

The moral of this section of the story is: It's really good to get some prac-tice with all of your chakras so that you don't quite make the scene that we made and you have the men guffawing behind their sword hands at you while the queen is there smelling really nice, and did we say she has pretty skin? The pretty-skin queen. We haven't even gotten around to why she's asked us here. She certainly didn't ask us here so we could get all weak in the knees about her. Or maybe she did. Because, after all, there's no king. The thing to focus on is that you have chakras that can make you go weak in the knees. When you get practice balancing out your chakras, you're going to feel more solid, more confident, more safe, more secure—what-ever word you like. Don't overlook the chakras that you are not strong in. Now is the time to let them have some air. Now is the time to work with them. Now is the time to be in them. It's important. Because really you can't be Homo spiritus unless you're balanced. This is a key of the ascen-sion process.

We're just going to take a bath. And normally, we're all excited about the girl who draws the bath. Not this time. Not this time. We are officially smitten. Officially smitten by the queen.

Twenty-seven

We went off to take a bath. Because we're not completely stupid yet, we did post the men in their secret places to listen in. We're smitten, but we're not idiots. Then we went to see the queen, Marianna. We show up to see the queen and we're concerned about our appearance. It's just so much easier when you come in muddy. However, we care what she thinks about us. There's the truth being expressed. We see her looking beautiful—we're not going to go into it—we want to show that we can be clean and actually have our clothing somewhat in non-disarray. So, there we are looking in the mirror and the truth of us is that we wish to present a certain appearance and it's not an appearance we normally care about. Normally, we want to look mean, tough, strong—bad-ass is the way you say it—and so it's how many pointy things can we strap to our body all at once and still be able to move and not clank too much? Instead now we're just trying to figure out if this belt goes with this sword or some shit like that, so we're going to skip forward a little bit because this is embarrassing and we need to get on with the story.

We show up at her—you know, they have these ridiculous little tables when they're queens. It's a ridiculous little table. It has curly legs and we think, "Oh, we're going to get it dirty." The table has claws on the legs and there are these ridiculous little cups to drink from. We can hardly even hold this little cup with our hands without smooshing it flat. There's so much to think about when you express the truth of you, there is much more stimulus; when you really are conscious in the moment there's so much more stimulus. When you have an interaction with things that you previously took for granted, there's so much more stimulus. It's all an op-portunity for you to know more about you. We are bitching about it, but we're learning how to hold a teacup and that's something new, so there you go. Learning something new about us. She's cute because we can't do the little handle so she graciously shows us how to turn the cup around and hold it a little bit more like we're used to. She's nice that way.

So, we're there and she's there and we're talking and the men are listening and we're happy about that and completely dismayed at the same time. She does that thing, damn it, you women, how do you know this, she just lays one beautiful hand on our arm. Unnerved, unnerved, by the gentle touch of a woman. What the hell! There she is being beautiful with the cups and the hand on the arm thing and we think, "OK, get your shit together, get back in certainty." That is the urge.

Here is the moment. The whole story, at least this section, comes down to this moment. We want to fall back into certainty. Where is certainty? Certainty is gruff, blustery, mud, farting, breaking the little teacup just because we can, that's certainty. Certainty is the men. Certainty is the dog. Certainty is Cedric. Certainty is the spear. Certainty is the sword. It's the sharpness. It's the pointy. All that is certainty. All that is strength. Everything we are known for, we want to fall back into that. We want to come off to her like, "Your hand on our arm, your stupid table, all your dumb little glasses and your beautifulness, forget all that crap, who do you want us to kill?" But we don't do that. We suck it up and we abide in the uncertainty of the moment in order to have the experience being offered with the cups and the table and the beautifulness. We look at her, we really look at her, and we see she is so delicate. We could reach out and with the smallest effort end her life. You have no idea how easy it would be. Like snapping a twig. It would be the smallest inconsequential act, it would be like if you had an ant on your hand and you just flicked it off, like you do. Not even as much effort as it would take to swat a fly, the flicking off of a gnat or an ant. She would be dead. It would take nothing. Yet here she is, completely holding us in her thrall. We are completely disarmed by her. How? Because she's just being the truth of herself, you see. This is why she has this power.

We have seen women before. Trust us. This is not the first girl. It's not even the first queen. But she stands here, or sits as the case may be, and she's very pretty—did we say that?—she sits here and she's just speaking her truth.

You know what her truth is? She knows that her vulnerability is evident but she's not afraid of it. It's alluring in such a powerful way. It's the most aphrodisiac thing we've ever experienced. The truth emanated without fear. In her case the truth being that she knows not only is she physically at our mercy if we chose, but her kingdom could be snapped out from under her at any second. Yet, she can sit in that uncertainty and in that truth and just speak to us knowing all those things. How does she do it?

How can she sit there? We don't know how she does it because, you see, we've always relied upon our wits and our strength and she sits there in her truth and feels unassailable. The honest thing is that truth is unassailable and we've talked to you about this before. But we've never seen it physicalized. We don't even care if that's a word. We've never seen it physicalized, yet that is what she can do. She is sitting there across the table from us unassailable and alluring as hell. At any moment we could just snap her life away, yet she feels more powerful than we are and we want to know how she does this. So, we think we'll be settling in for a little bit. For so many good reasons. The men want to rest and it's kind of cold outside. Cedric and his dog need a place just to hang out and get to know each other. We're lying. We don't give a shit about any of that right now.

All we want to do is learn from her how she can be that vulnerable and that strong at the same time.

Twenty-eight

We're still having tea. She hasn't told us anything. We haven't told her anything. We're just busy thinking about how soft her skin must be. So, we're going to speed this up a little.

As it turns out there never was a king. She's not a widow. We thought for sure she had to be a widow. How did she keep it secret for this long? Her father was the king. Her father died, not her husband. This wasn't something that was talked about because it was a source of perceived weakness that there was no king. This is a period of time when women weren't exactly having equal rights. So, there is no king and she's not a widow and we find that fascinating because she really has held it together. She really has. She hasn't had to wage any wars or do much about that and the place where her castle and lands are—castle, it's not what you think of as a castle but we are calling it a castle because we're enamored of her. It's not nice to call your hopeful lady friend's house a shack, so we're just going to call it a castle for now. It could use some improvements, but the truth of the matter is this place that she stays in is reinforced and it is a place that has been protected over the years and it is a place where they have had a lineage of royalty that are in charge of a certain amount of land but they are kind of off to the side a bit. No one much messes with them and no one much communicates with them because the whole community turned inward when the king died without a male heir. But she's pretty badass herself and she stepped up and said, "Look, I'm going to be in charge." The people hemmed and hawed, but the bottom line is no one else wanted the job. Kind of. There's always somebody out there who wants the job, if you know what we mean, but people liked her and they respected her and they decided, "Well, we'll just see how it goes." It's been going along for less than a year, but she knew the story was going to get out really soon and she thought she might like to have, let's say, some folks that are good with the third chakra around just in case the neighboring king and his sons, of which there are plenty, decided to come around and say, "By the way, you better marry one of these boys because we're going to take you over if you don't."

She thought, "Well, I'll just call these guys that run around in the forest all the time, have them come hang out with me, and if these guys come around there'll be a little bit of a buffer, and at least maybe perhaps we can make it a negotiation rather than being forced." But as it turns out, her little heart is going aflutter, aflutter, as well. Oh, hell. She kind of likes the looks of us. There's plenty to look at. If she likes to look at us and we like to look at her, well, maybe we should become a little more friendly. It's all well and good to get all worked up in the heart chakra and it's all well and good to get worked up in the second chakra and we certainly know how to do that, but what ends up happening now is it gets really complicated. Because you don't take a queen that doesn't have a king that might be getting taken over by the neighboring kingdom, you don't just jump into bed with a woman like that. Even we know that. She's not that kind of girl and we don't mean she's a prude. We mean she knows that she has to play it real close to the chest here because this is a chess match and her people's future depends on it.

She likes the look of us, sure. She likes the fact that we have our men. God help us, she even likes the dog. We thought the dog would scare her. We have to backtrack because we thought the dog would scare her. Because remember, five feet tall, three heads. We thought the dog would kind of scare her. There we are, we've had our tea and we've gone out and we've seen to the men, and we've made sure everybody's doing OK and there are horses to attend to and Cedric, of course, is taking care of that very nicely, and we're walking with her out into this courtyard area and who comes galumphing along? Riley. Remember he slobbers? She's not big. She's seeing eye to eye with this five-foot-tall, three-headed, slobbering dog with a tail. That's a lot of slobber. We thought for sure he was going to upset her and we thought we were going to have to step in and we were being in the future slightly. Why? Because we really wanted to control the outcome because we really want her to like the damn dog because we like her.

Here comes the dog, galumph, happy to see us, and she's there, off to the side and Riley doesn't exactly see her and here he comes and he wants to say hi to us and she steps out to see what the commotion is and he's sliding to a stop with his legs and the slobber and he slobbers on her and we think oh, this is it. She's going to be so mad. What does she do? She laughs. She laughs at the dog slobber. Then she says, "Does he fetch?" It's not enough that the dog runs, skids, gets her dirty, and slobbers on her. Now, she wants to know, if she throws the stick, will he do it some more? Will he do it some more? What kind of woman is this? Where does she come from? She doesn't mind the slobbering, three-headed dog? Now here comes Cedric around the corner looking chagrined because, of course, Riley is his responsibility. We've told you Cedric is young and he's gangly like the dog and he has pointy things hanging off of him and has dog slobber and dirt all over him. We're not making the best impression with our family. We have a gangly teenager and slobbering dog and of course what does she do? She asks him questions about the dog and then Cedric has to show that he can ride Riley and then it becomes a whole thing where everybody wants to come and watch and we're thinking she's just about as perfect as a woman can be. What the hell are we going to do now? We're just about ready to burst. What would you do?

What do you do when it's there? It's right there in your hand. It's the thing you've always wanted. The thing that looks perfect. You know, of course, it's not perfect but it looks damn fine. You think, "Do I deserve it? Can I have it? Can I let myself stretch this far? Can I open up? Can I be that big? Could I be a king? Could I really have a family?" And the "could I just fill in the blank," whatever your current blank is? What is your blank? It's very fun to tell this story but until it ties back to you it's irrelevant. "Could I? Could I stand up into that? Could I allow it? What's the static between it and me?" Right now, we could very easily say, "Let's go back and live in the trees, me and the boys and the dog. We want to go out and do our thing, chasing dragons." Stay small. Stay the same. Do the same things you've always done. Or what if instead of that, you took the chance to be that little bit more, or the heck of a lot more, what if you did that?

Well, you know what we're going to do? We're going to make some babies with this woman. Are you kidding? As soon as humanly possible. We want to make babies with this woman or else the story would be pretty boring. For us, too. The woods are not looking good at this point, we'll tell you that right now. The village of good food is far from here. So, stick your head up and see what happens. Be in uncertainty. What's going to happen when the boys next door come over and find that not only is the Queen smitten but betrothed. Or maybe we should just hurry it up. We don't know. We'll see how the story goes. But what happens when Mr. King and six of his boys come over all wondering who's going to have a shot at her and instead of finding Marianna and her village, he finds us, the men, the dog, and the kid and all the sharp things we like to carry with us. It would be easier just to go back into the forest, don't you think?

We've never fought for what we wanted, really. It's never been about us, necessarily. It's always been sort of a bigger picture that we just popped in and out of. Sound familiar? What about when the story's all you? Sound familiar? Sound like your life these days?

We're a little bit over the initial overwhelm of the fourth chakra turning on for the first time. Well, actually, Cedric turned it on for the first time. Seeing Cedric with the dog and watching him throw the knife in the tree. Remember when we told you about Cedric throwing the knife in the tree? That's when the fourth chakra turned on. We thought, "Oh, God," but we didn't tell you that because we were playing it cool but then when Marianna showed up, we knew there was no way we could hide it from you.

Twenty-nine

The neighboring king has five sons. Gustav and the gang of guys. Here they come. We're fast-forwarding a little. First, we have to say this. We've been around for a little while now and this smitten thing has really taken and we're patching walls and we have the men teaching the other men how to defend the kingdom. Cedric has completely taken over the stables and he has them all straightened out and all the animals are doing real well.

One night, we decide we're going to have dinner with the guys, our guys, and so we gather them all up and we look at each of them in the eye and we say, "Well, imagine this. Imagine what's happened now." We look around at each of them and realize that we were emanating the truth of our experience. This is the truth of us. We're here with Marianna, we're kind of digging this lady a huge amount, we have the kid, we have the dog, she needs some help, and this is a pretty cool place, and so we're feeling like we're going to stick around here for a while. What we're wondering is how is the truth of you presented here? Basically what we're going to say right now is if you want to go, you can. Because up until this point we were all kind of a band and now we're saying if you want to go, you can. The current truth we are experiencing is the now we want to be in, and the life that we had before where we were running around in the forest and talking to dragons and stuff, that's not the now we want to experience at this moment.

This is hard for us to do because it brings up the idea of lack. What if these men don't stay with us and what if we need them and they're gone? But we respect them enough to ask them to emanate their truth. That's part of what you do is when you have made a decision about emanating your truth: you respect the ones around you enough to emanate theirs and occasionally that means you can't be in relationship anymore. "What is my truth here? What is your truth here?" It's kind of heavy. Here we are with the guys and we say, "Yo, guys, so what do you say? What do you want to do? We're going to stick around here for a while, we've decided. We've been invited to stay. She needs us. We need her. The kid and the dog like it here. This looks like the place we want to hang out. What do you guys think?" Ten of them say, you know what? We like it here too. It's interesting to be useful in a new way. It's interesting to have a bed to sleep in. It's interesting to not be out in the snow. We kind of like the gals or the guys, whatever they're into, we don't care, and we are interested in—actually, a lot of them are very interested in teaching. You wouldn't think it to look at them because they're just a bunch of gruff guys. They don't smell as bad these days but they're big, gruff guys. But there comes a time when you've made it through enough battles that you either turn really hard or you say, "I made it through because there's something I have to offer to another." So, ten of them say we're going to stick around with you if we can. And, of course, we say, yes you can. And the rest of them say, look, we're not leaving, but we're not telling you we're staying, either. It's hard because then there's uncertainty. Are they going to go? When are they going to go? Why would they go? Don't they love us? You've felt this a little? Are they going to go tomorrow? Are they going to go the next day? Will they go as soon as the fighting starts? Uncertainty, uncertainty, uncertainty.

Now, you can see in our story how ridiculous it is to even think about that. Will they leave tomorrow? What about when we have to cut down the hay? Will they be here for that? It's one thing to say we need the help but it's quite another thing to fuss about that when they're still sitting here right in front of us. Yet you do it all the time. You're in a relationship, you're in a friendship, you're in a business relationship. Will it end? Will it end? You can see how silly it is to miss out on the moment because you're worried about it ending.

We've talked to the men. We feel better now that we talked to the men because we've said our truth and we've made it clear. Remember Eric and how he never did that and the problems that caused? OK, we're not going to repeat Eric's mistakes. So fast-forward, fast-forward. It's been about three months now, everything's really cool, no, we're not officially the king yet but boy, howdy, what else do you need to do to get that job? Apparently, get married, but we're not going to talk about that right now. We're patching holes in walls and we're teaching kids to throw knives. Do you have any idea how much stuff goes on in a castle? It's just crazy. But it's all good. Anyway, we are liking it. We're not complaining. Tired at night but look who's in bed with us. No complaints here. Moving along.

All of a sudden, Gustav and his gang of guys decide to come over and pay a visit. Now, the thing is Gustav has kind of heard a little rumor that old Queenie isn't necessarily as available as she once was. This is a problem because old Gustav has had his eye on the castle and Marianna and the land that she holds and all that crap. He's suspected there wasn't a king around for a little while, and even before, he suspected that there was a chance that this could work out for one of his five sons, so he decides to come for a visit.

Now, when this guy comes for a visit, the problem is it's extremely hard to not feel threatened. He rides up with all his guys and his kids and his horses and his sharp pointy things and banners and fancy clothes and all that crap, and we're out there, of course, working in the fields and all sweaty and dirty and doing what we do and taking care of things and up comes this guy. Now, what's very interesting and maybe surprising about this story, and this will tell you just how smitten we are if you didn't already know, we had a little bit of insecurity. Look at that! There are six of them to choose from, or five. Again, it's hard to tell. They're all blonde. It's like popcorn. They just all look the same.

They ride up on their pretty horses—they have some nice animals—and Cedric is over there gawking—we'll have to talk to the boy about gawking at the guys who make us feel jealous—there's no gawking! They have all the nice clothes that we usually make fun of and all that stuff. They kind of make a show. Of course, they come today of all days because we have our sleeves rolled up and we're sweaty and dirty and we're standing in mud and shoveling something that smells bad but it's good for something. We don't even know what we're doing at this point, but it's really stinky and of course here they come in all their blondness and good horses and pretty clothes and they don't stink and Cedric is looking at them and all the men and the women are looking at them and then there's Marianna and you know what? She's being nice to them. Of course she has to be. It's her job as a queen. You have to be nice to the other guy because he might stab you if you're not. We're standing there thinking, is she going to change her mind? Is she going to change her mind because now the pretty boys have come into town? This is a thought unworthy of us. But we're having it nonetheless, and we're sharing it with you because the heart chakra got turned on and this is one of the things that comes along with that. Damn it. That sense of: Shit, we're not just smitten with this chick. We're in love with her and we want her to love us back. Then there are the pretty boys with the popcorn hair and we are in the mud and what if she changes her mind? There's some uncertainty for you. But the key here that we want you to know *is the uncertainty is within us*. She's not expressing any uncertainty to us. We haven't even talked to her since the popcorn boys showed up. All we know is that looking at her and looking at Cedric looking at their horses we think: uncertainty.

Uncertainty, you have to be really cautious about it because sometimes it comes from a place that you project onto other people but it has nothing to do with them. If we think that our uncertainty is her fault then we're going to be mad at her, when really the truth is it's coming from within. Do you get it? You do this all the time. So be careful that you take responsibility for your uncertainty because it's the portal of Homo spiritus and all that. Yeah, yeah, we get that. But on a very earthy level it's your responsibility because it's your creation, too, and it's your responsibility because it creates interaction with your life. We're not going to be this stupid, but what if we felt jealous and dirty and stinky and we yelled at her. "How dare you be nice to them?" Or whatever, because we felt diminished. It's a good thing we're going to take care of that inside rather than take it out on her because we don't want to be a stereotype.

The popcorn boys want to stay for a couple of nights so that means we have to find a place for them to sleep. We figure that out. No problem. Cedric is still drooling over their damn horses. It's hard to improve the stock of beasties in this time we're sharing the story from. It's really hard. To make a new horse takes a while and to get a good stud and a good mare together when the world is so spread out is really hard. So, if you're kind of working with not-so-great stock to begin with, it takes a very long time to build up a really nice stable. Cedric came from the other kingdom with that other guy. Remember the one that we threw down? He had really nice animals because he was a more established king. Marianna hasn't been paying so much attention to the horses. So, we don't blame Cedric. He's not mad at us for not giving him good horses. He just sees, "Wow, if I take this one over here and get this horse lucky tonight. They won't know. Go to sleep, I'm going to get your horse lucky." That's the kind of thing that Cedric is thinking. But when we see the admiration in his eyes for something we can't give him, the choice could be to feel diminished by that, again, instead of seeing the truth of it which is the discomfort, the uncertainty. We know what the child wants and we can't give it to him. We sit in that discomfort. We can't give it to him yet. Someday, maybe. But we can give him all that we have to give and there's a lot to be learned from what you cannot give someone else. Old Cedric, he's so smart, because he's just going to go get it himself. He's got this horse and that horse and there's all kind of sex happening in the stables, we'll tell you that right now. Cedric is a man with a mission at this point. He's a smart kid.

Really watch where the uncertainty that you feel is self-generated—and it can be called jealousy, it can be called envy, it can be called feeling diminished or not having confidence in yourself. There are different words, you understand. We go and walk a little closer to Marianna. We're certainly not going to walk up there and swing our shlang and say, "Hey, this is ours." We have some pride, after all. So we kind of sidle up a little closer and she catches sight of us and she just smiles! How do you women do that? How do you know how to do that? How do you know how to look at a man and smile and make him feel 20 feet tall? Do you know you have that power? You have that power to just smile in a way that makes us go [deep sigh].

She calls us over and we shake hands with the popcorn crowd and, of course, now everybody's gathered around because this is like the Super Bowl. Mr. what's-his-head and six friends come over with all their pageantry. This is the closest thing to the Super Bowl that we get in our time. She says, "This is my beloved." Holy God in heaven. What the hell just happened? "This is my beloved." Right there. In front of all of them. We ain't going no place. Nothing is dragging us out of this joint.

Thirty

There she is looking radiant, and there are all the popcorn boys, most of them looking pretty good, too. There we are standing in cow crap, but even when you're stuck in the shit of your life, literally or figuratively, you can still emanate your truth. Even when you're confused, even when you find yourself sensing limitation, which is a little bit like where we're tempted to go, to feel slightly limited. On the field of battle or out in the forest or in many, many situations we have absolutely no hesitation to confidence, but here we're in a different field of battle. In essence we're in the field of the battle of the heart and we're a beginner, such a beginner. She stands there and she's so good at it. The popcorn boys are here and we're a little bit unstable, we're a little bit not our balanced self.

You know how this feels, so what do we do? The first thing is to acknowledge the confidence that she's showing in us. She's telling us the truth of us, she's showing us, she's reminding us, "This is the truth of you. I know you don't feel quite like that right now, it doesn't matter, I know the truth of you. Yeah you have some shit on your boots, you actually smell pretty horrid right now, but I know the truth of you, I know who you are. I see who you are and I'm going to stand here and witness the truth of who you are in front of anyone who cares to walk near you." So, it helps a little. That's where you support each other and you remind each other of the truth of you and this is where having connection to your soul's perspective is very helpful because your soul's perspective says, "Hey, you're infinite and immortal. You just feel like you're standing in shit right now, but it's not always going to be like this."

OK, so we told you the story about how Cedric very quickly whisked their horses away—mostly so he could get his mares with foal as quickly as possible, hopefully with no one noticing. He's a bright boy, that one. Did we tell you about them meeting the dog? Oh boy, well, there's something that makes you feel like a man when your three-headed, five-foot tall, dog comes around the corner. It sure confused the popcorn boys! It was so hilarious. Here comes Riley—slobbering, of course—and we got him to sit right down next to us.

You have your beautiful woman and you might be standing in a little bit of shit and you have your three-headed, five-foot tall, dog and he's sitting there like he knows what to do, and secretly you're quite amazed that he behaves. It's like, yes, luck held, the dog listened. Cedric's been doing a really good job with him. That was kind of impressive and it broke the tension a little bit. It also put these boys on notice that things are not as they expected them to be.

We'll fast-forward now. We've had our dinner and after dinner, while having some wine, it comes down to it.

Mr. King, despite Marianna's proclamation that we are her beloved, decides to make his play. He decides to make his play right there in front of us. We thought, well, he's got some balls on him that guy there. He says, "I have five boys," or six, no one seems to be able to keep track, "which one do you want?" Now, it's very difficult when you're trying to live as the truth of you to have someone demean you to that level. It's demeaning; it is demeaning to imply that her only value is as meat. We didn't particularly like that, we mostly didn't like it because he's basically ignoring that fact that we're sitting there. But the other part of it that we didn't like more was that it was as though the work she had done to manage the kingdom and the work she had done to build up the confidence of her people and the work she had done to be the beautiful, truthful version of her was all irrelevant. All that really matters is that she's breeding stock. Even Cedric isn't as callous with his mares.

We might have to do something about this, it could be a problem. This could be a problem in a big way. You know why? Because really right about now all we want to do is stab this guy. He's sort of pissed us off. Then we think, God damn it, we really are besotted with this woman because we're thinking about stabbing a king. It's one thing to throw down a king that you've known a long time like we did at the other castle, that king respects us, he knows us. This dude is acting like he's never heard of us, which pisses us off, and he's got five or six boys that probably can stab back. How do you get out of this situation? As it turns out, we didn't have to do anything. Mariana simply says, "I am already betrothed." As if we had had the balls to ask—because we actually hadn't, but you didn't hear us say that and if you repeat it we will find something sharp and make you familiar with it very quickly. She says, "I'm already betrothed," and we just about crap.

Now remember, back in the day at some other village, we told you that at some point the guys all get out their knives and start to sharpen them? Yeah, every single one of them, all thirteen. They're starting to sharpen and we think, woo, you know those relationships you create by being the truth of you? You can lean into those at times. Because, you know what? Thirteen is more than five, six, or seven. Boy, are we glad they stuck around.

Now, Mr. King and all of his popcorn-headed boys are not all that interested in passing on this opportunity to take over her lands and to be able to control the west-facing entrance to his lands. All that crap, you know, really we're just trying to get some fields ploughed now; we don't care about the rest of it. But they really care. They don't particularly care that we're betrothed because you see, they assume we're expendable—and in their minds we are. Since they haven't heard of us, that's one of those things. You know, it pisses us off that they haven't heard of us but guess what? They don't know who we are. They don't know the truth of us. Having thirteen men all pull out their knives and sharpen them simultaneously makes a statement, so Mr. King backs down for now, but we have a strong suspicion we haven't heard the last of him. And we have a stronger suspicion that this marriage is going to happen pretty damn soon.

How the hell did we get here? Wasn't it just a little while ago that we were romping through the forest wondering if it was a dragon or not, and now we have a kid, a dog, a wife, and a whole community to feed. How did this happen? You know how it happened. Life is full of infinite possibilities and it's time for balance. What was missing before? Well, love, of course. Right? Love was missing before.

Here we are with an opportunity to create even deeper balance, because it's not only balance within but balance with her, balance with Cedric, balance with the damn dog, balance with the men, balance with feelings. It's the opportunity to take the expression of ourselves into and through new experiences.

As you open up to the field of infinite possibilities and you start to frolic—watch out, you might end up with a wife, kid, and a dog! Could happen. As you frolic out there in your field of infinite possibilities, new stuff is going to happen. That's what infinite possibilities means. New stuff is going to happen and then what do you do? You take the truth of you, your balanced nature, all your tools, and your relationships into that new space.

Thirty-one

What have we done? It is not honorable to run away. It is not honorable to run away and if you want to talk all about balance, balance, balance, balance, balance, then this whole heart chakra thing is probably important. Crap. All right. Here we are at our wedding. So, we have to back up just a bit. This is the deal.

We spent a very, very long time running around with sharp things doing whatever felt fun at the moment. You know, there comes a time when you're ready to try something else, and we didn't know when we showed up here that was going to be now, but as it turns out, it is. Now is the time for everything we know and everything we have within us to have an opportunity to be emanated in this space. Previously, we sort of just passed through town and that was fun, but there's a sense that we're ready to make an investment, an investment in our emanation, an investment in sharing our tools and abilities and our perspective and our outlook and our willingness. This heart chakra thing started up and boy, is she pretty. She just does that smile thing and it's all over with. So, guess what? We want to be here. We're not going to be ashamed to admit that it feels a little knight-in-shining-armor and we kind of dig that. We're not afraid to admit that.

Here she comes along and she has this amazing presence. We wish you could meet her. She has this amazing presence and then she shines it on us and it's like, really? Honest to God. OK. We see a place here. We see a place where we can fit it. We shovel some horseshit and we build a few walls and we spend a little more time drinking tea out of those ridiculous cups and we look at her and she is so generous of spirit and we think: That's something we'd like to learn. How do you be that generous of spirit? How can you give without giving up anything? How do you give without falling into service? The truth really is that her emanation is so genuine and pure she lights the room. We haven't done that. We haven't lit the room. We've pissed people off and we've lit the room up, but we haven't lit the room with the truth of us. She knows something that we don't know, and we want to know it. We want to know how she can be so powerful. How can she be that powerful in that little bitty body with those pretty dresses and those ridiculous teacups? She has all these ribbons. We haven't told you about her ribbons, have we? She has these ribbons and they're always in her hair. We haven't told you what she looks like, either. She has dark hair and she has these ribbons and she wears them in her hair. Occasionally, we find them places. We don't know if she does this on purpose. We suspect she does. We find them places. Well, of course she leaves them, but it's hard to believe she would leave them where we found them. The other day we found one on the horse. It was tied in the mane of the horse.

She has these ribbons and she leaves them about. We have a whole collection of them now. It's just ridiculous. We can't believe we're saying this out loud. She lights up the room with the truth of her and therefore we want to be with her. As it turns out, she can use us. Not just use us because we're strong and scary, but she could use us the way we can use her in the sense that is too hard to be a queen without a king at this time. Not because she's a woman, but because of the way society is set up. She's perfectly capable of running her kingdom or queendom by herself. Society doesn't let her. Can you imagine how frustrating that must be to know you're capable and not be given the opportunity? The truth of her cannot be emanated in society without help, and all you have to have is a penis to help that. So, we have one. That was an easy job to fill. But beyond that, beyond all of that, there's the heart chakra connection that happened. And we'll say the second chakra connection followed very quickly.

Then we found out there was a place for us, and that's really the point we're trying to make. Not only was there a need for us, but there was a place for us and that's the distinction we want to be clear about. She needed someone to help her solidify her hold on her kingdom in a society that requires a king, but there was a place for us, where? In her heart. Because we're not going to just sign up to be a king for any old person. Are you kidding? You know how we feel about kings. You think we want to do that job just for anybody? Hell, no. You're clear on that, right? We haven't lost you in this whole mushy story with ribbons and all that?

She has a place for us, we're just telling you, so we're not just doing it for the hell of it. We're not just doing it because we like getting in the sack with her or whatever. We're doing it because she has something we want to learn about, she needs us, which we enjoy, and we know we need her. It is time to emanate the truth rather than just run around with the truth. Rather than just running through villages, it's time to stay close to one place, and consistently show the truth of us to others. Some of you do the same thing. You run through friendships, you run through jobs, you run through relationships, and is the truth of you actually known or is it just sort of skimmed? Sometimes holding still, and this doesn't necessarily mean settling down for everyone, but holding still within yourself requires a deeper assessment of the truth of you than moving quickly does.

In come the popcorn kids and they're pretty sure one of these six guys is going to marry her because, well, she's going to do what they say because this is how society works. She says, "Oh, here is my beloved, betrothed,"—it's always so overwhelming when she does that— and then it becomes really clear that there has to be a wedding really soon, witnessed by these guys so they know she's not bullshitting them. All of a sudden it becomes beloved, betrothed, holy crap, we're having a wedding.

The guy from next door, we know he's going to be trouble down the road, just wait, he says, "Oh great, when's the wedding?" That kind of crap. A guy like that would just be easier to stick with our sword but if we do, we'll have even more problems, so we can't solve it that way. He tries to call her on the carpet. That pisses us off. We told you all the guys are sharpening their knives, all 13 of them simultaneously. It's like a symphony orchestra. You would love this. How they can do that all together as if there's a conductor? Can you imagine? All 13 of them. Cedric is in the stables with the horses screwing each other like crazy. He told us, "I'm not coming to dinner; I'm not doing anything until this is all taken care of." The rest of them are doing their knives.

The guy says, "When's the wedding?" Because he's trying to catch her out. "Tomorrow." We were the one that said "tomorrow," by the way, because we're in for a penny, in for a pound, isn't that how they say it? Shit. So, it's the night before and we've said tomorrow and that means the wedding is coming very, very quickly, and all the men are very carefully, very carefully, laughing at us. They know that we've been pushed into a corner and they know they had to get out their knives and do their symphony of sharpening, but that is not going to hold them back from giving us all the shit they think they can without getting stabbed. They're laughing but they're happy. Then we have to drink a bunch of whatever there is to drink because we're having the equivalent of a bachelor party, but we know if we get shitfaced we're going to be in big trouble the next day. Plus, we have to keep in mind these popcorn guys might decide to do something here. We don't know. They might decide that they don't like us marrying Marianna.

So, now it's the morning, and we're supposed to get married. We've laid out our best clothes, we've actually bathed and combed our hair and put some braids down the side, we have only have our best sharp stuff on, and we're all ready to go. All the men are with us. Now, what's interesting—we have no idea why when you get married you have groomsmen but we sure as hell know why we do. Because if we didn't have 13 guys with lots of sharpness and muscles, these dudes would whack us and marry her in our place. You get it?

Can you imagine? There you are all nervous and sort of hung over, just a teeny bit though, a little hung over and you're thinking, "There's five or six of them sitting out there and they might try to kill me during the wedding. And holy crap, I'm getting married!" Think of that all at the same time, why don't you? No wonder you go on a honeymoon after. We'll tell you right now, we got married facing the crowd. You guys all get married with your backs to the crowd. Hell, no. We'd never do that. We get married facing the crowd. Why? Because we wanted all our guys looking at them. The threat is not from the preacher man. The threat is from the crowd. Talk about a tough crowd! There's a tough crowd for you! The whole time we're wondering, "Are they going to whack us?"

You want to know what she is wearing, don't you? Of course you do. If you didn't, we'd be shocked. So, there we are and it's outside because it's a nice day. We didn't tell you about that part, either, but it's a nice day so we decided to have it outside because why have it inside when you can have it outside on a nice day? So, we're outside, it's a nice day, and there we are standing with all our guys. Just imagine, 13 of them; and Cedric is going to come to the wedding, don't worry. He's taking a break from all the horse sex to come to the wedding. So we have 13 guys, us facing the crowd, and then off from over there Cedric's leading her on one of the horses and she's there and the horse is white and she's got the dark hair and she's wearing a very pretty gown that's sort of a light color. It's not white. But there she is on the horse with the hair and Cedric is leading the horse. Of course, the dog is here but he's kind of tied up off to the side because, no, the dog can't come to the wedding. Here she comes. She just glows and she doesn't look at anyone but us. We're telling you, died and gone to heaven all in one, and stuck around, too.

She's looking at us and you know what the beauty is? Because we have 13 guys taking care of our back, we can look at her. If we ever enjoyed the investment we made in all of those relationships more, we can't tell you when it was. Not when we fought the dragon, not when we were running from the other king, in none of those other stories that we've told you, have we ever known our back was completely covered enough to take our attention off the potential enemy and enjoy the moment to the extreme in this way. You know what's awesome, is when we reach up and we lift her off of the horse. It is like no one else is here. Don't know if we'll ever feel this way again, but boy, does it feel good.

There we are, looking in her eyes, and the kid is over there, and the dog is somewhere and all that, and the men are there looking after our back. Our back's to our men, our eyes to the woman, it's a very powerful place to be. It's a very powerful place. It's a little bit like the past and the future, too. With our backs to the men, they've been our past, and eyes to the future. But it's all in the moment as well. It's a very interesting sort of set of circumstances.

The preacher man's here and she says, "Will you stand beside me and care for my people with me? Will you hold me? Will you know me? Will you love me? As I do for you." God damn, it is just over in that moment. Knees just turned to Jell-O and they wiggle. We've never wiggled in our knees. Are you kidding? "Ah, yeah." That's basically all we can say and we're not ashamed to admit it. You wouldn't do any better. Guaranteed, none of you, even you fifth-chakra people could do any better. You would've just gone, "uh-huh. Thank God I'm me right now." Then she says, "OK, that's good enough for me." About then, we decided we probably should take a look at the popcorn guys and it seems they have decided that that was all well and good for now, and that was a good choice because we outnumber them two to one. Plus, they're on our turf and all their horses are really tired, so it doesn't matter. They're not getting far. Now Cedric's got a mom. He's pretty damn happy about that. He hasn't had one of those in his memory. We're going to make some babies with her. We'll tell you that right now.

Thirty-two

The vows are said and holy crap we're married in holy matrimony. Is holy matrimony holy crap? We think that might go together somehow. We're not real sure about how you do it but we were thinking holy crap as we got linked up in holy matrimony because we didn't see this one coming, not for a long, long time. Then we said the, "OK, I do," and all that, and we're officially married. By the way, that makes us the king, and, shit, what does that even mean? They want to put something on our head, we don't care, because the whole time we're kind of looking at her and we're trusting the men to look at the other guys and now it's catching up to us. It's catching up to us that this has all happened and, boy, you want to talk about uncertainty. Like oh, wow we have a kid and a wife and the men and a kingdom, small as it may be. You have to remember here, this is a very humble kingdom that we have just married into. It's not huge by any means. For the time, it's pretty impressive enough, but it's not anything like you've seen in fairy tales with all the turrets and stuff. Don't be confused. Give us time. We have plans already, but right now, there's a gate. It's nice to have a gate. Gates are good when you're living in our time.

Here we are, and now we're going to have a feast because of course you have to have a party after a wedding. This is when we start to really worry and by worry we mean get wary. Wary, because just because we're married to her doesn't mean we're out of danger yet. It doesn't mean she's out of danger, either. Because there is some thought that if we were the king trying to take over, we might just kill both of us. There is no baby. There's no heir. What are the peasants going to do? Honestly, what are the peasants going to do? Not a damn thing. They can't.

Here's the situation. Now we recognize that we aren't just in mortal danger ourselves, but they want to kill our queen. That's pissing us off real bad, real bad. So we have 13, they have six or seven and they have their hangers-on and stuff, but really we don't have to worry too much about any of those guys. Basically, we have them 2 to 1 with home turf advantage, not so impressive, but it's making it hard to celebrate. It's making it hard to celebrate. Then Cedric comes around the corner. Somebody has given Cedric a black eye. Oh, boy. This is not good. Cedric walks up to us and he's trying real hard not to let us see the black eye because he doesn't want to break up the perfect little image of his new family, you see. You get it? He wants control over the environment. And who wouldn't? You have to remember he's 13 or 14, something in that range. He doesn't have any parents. This is the closest he's ever had to family. He doesn't want to screw it up. But because he's a smart kid and he knows we'll find out anyway and it's better if it comes from him, he comes to us right away.

Now we are tempted to have all kinds of thoughts running through our head about who, what, when, why and where has Cedric gotten this black eye, and we sit here, wondering which avenue we should. So, he comes to us and he says something ridiculous like, "Your Majesty." Because he's used to living with the other king and he's afraid. See, he's afraid because he's uncertain now and he's uncertain in an unconscious way. He's uncertain if he's done something wrong and that somehow all this perfect little picture—imagine, he goes from being an orphan and overlooked in this other kingdom, barely making it, barely having food, sleeping with the horses. It's only because he's good with the beasties that he even has a life to call his own. We scoop him up into our adventures, take him off, show him what it's like to be a man, include him in all of our stuff, teach him how to throw the knives and shoot the crossbows and all that stuff, get him the dog, and now he's got a mom or he thinks she could be his mom, at least she's his friend, and something has happened on our wedding night. He knows there's tension already because one of our guys took him aside and said, "Look don't be stupid here, keep yourself close by, stay near us," et cetera. But Cedric is uncertain and he's uncertain in the worst way. He's uncertain for his very safety.

When you're uncertain about your safety you act unconsciously because you go into very primal habitual behaviors. If you feel uncertain about your safety, be really careful about what you do next. Especially if you're not actually in danger. It's a real red flag. Here he comes, and he says, "Your Majesty," and he tries to bow or something and we feel like slapping him and giving him another black eye because that's just stupid shit there, and we say, "Are you kidding? We don't give a shit. We're going to talk about that later. What about this black eye?"

The black eye came from one of the other grooms-kids. They had to bring people with them because they have so many horses and stuff. One of the grooms-kids made a comment about the Queen. The comment was something along the lines of: "Well, she'll just marry any bit of trash that comes along," or something like that. He and Cedric got into what you might call a real drop-down, drag-out brawl about that. It wasn't just a scuffle. He gave as good as he got. As it turns out, this kid was a little more likely to be a smart-mouth and not a scrapper, so the kid's not doing so great. He's not going to die or anything but he's looking worse than Cedric. Cedric has such a heart in him that when he realizes he's kicked the shit out of this kid, he knows he has to get him help. So now, he's come to us to say, "I just kicked the crap out of this other guy and he's bleeding and I need your help because I don't know what to do." What a kid. More uncertainty. "I was afraid, I reacted, and now I have to clean up a mess." We're thinking this could just be the match on this little pile of kindling we have going. Mr. King from next door, we wonder: Do we have an unconscious king here or do we have a king that maybe we can make peace with? What do you do when you're in that circumstance? You confront the truth straight on.

We asked for silence in the hall. We stand up, pull Cedric next to us, and we say: "There's a story that needs to be told. And we expect Cedric to tell it." Now, you think about calling somebody or talking to somebody, can you imagine? Here you are, completely terrified that your whole way of life is changing and could go back to something worse and you're being asked to be a man in front of everyone. So, old Cedric is going to do it. And when you think about doing it, remember Cedric is only 13 and he's scared. What does he say? He's a good kid. He says, "The grooms-kid and I had a fight and I believe he's hurt and I'm sorry he's hurt. I did not mean to hurt him that badly. My temper got away from me. He needs care." And the men of the neighboring kingdom notice that not only did we not try to hide it, but that we spoke about it immediately, and that Cedric spoke about it with such frankness and such honesty that we earned some of their respect that day. Because if even our children are required to live that consciously and to stand up in that kind of manly way, you might call it, they know that our presence is not just, "Yeah, you're a big guy, so maybe you're dangerous." But they start to see, "Wait a second, this isn't just riffraff off the street that's come into this kingdom." Then, because Cedric is our son in all but biology, we say, "Mr. King, will you please accompany us to see about this boy?" We're going to go together to see about the children under our charge. We invite him to stand up from the table of celebration and take responsibility and be conscious about the boys having gotten into it. By this act we show him that we are comrades, not threats.

Really, why he wanted this kingdom—because it's not much, we've told you, there are no riches here—he wanted this kingdom so he could feel safe about the eastern flank to his lands being taken care of. And so one of his kids would get out of his hair. By showing him that we have integrity we showed him that he does not have to feel threatened by us. We answered his question of: "I'm unsure about this person." When you tell your truth, you help other people to be more sure about who you are and where you stand. When you're comfortable in uncertainty, you make it easier to be around you. When you're comfortable, you say, "I'm uncertain, but I'm going to tell the truth. I don't know how it's going to turn out, but rather than try to control it I'm going to tell the truth and trust myself to handle however it falls out."

The other king joins us and we go out, while Cedric runs ahead. Turns out the boy has a bloody nose and is a little woozy, but he's all right. The king says to us there, outside, away from the men—although ours are just over there, they're never going to leave us alone with this dude, especially since Cedric is here and we would have to look out for him if there were fighting. He says, "You know, I didn't know you, but I know you now, and I want you to be an ally. I want to collaborate and communicate well with you. We got off on the wrong foot. Just as your son is sorry that the fight went as far as it did, we are sorry that our getting off on the wrong foot with you went as far as it did. May we both now, the children and the two of us, come into a balance with each other about the fact that, yes, we got away from ourselves for a minute but the truth is we want to prosper, we want to protect and support our people, and we want to see our loved ones loved well."

The End

Epilogue

Remember, stand toe to toe with your enemies. You know why? You want to know what they know. You want to know how they smell. You want to know how they taste. You want to know if their hair is greasy, if they have dirt under their fingernails. You want to stand toe-to-toe, eye-to-eye. You want to give them a good sniff. You want to sense their truth and in that you will know, *you will know* their weaknesses.

Face the internal enemy. Face your triggers, your habits, and your patterns that don't serve you. Stand toe to toe with them so you will know them. Being afraid of something you do not know is unworthy of you! Do you hear us? Unworthy of you, to be afraid of something that you have not smelled up close. When you know it, when you feel it, when you smell it, then you will know how to attend to it. Get up close and you will see, "Ah, yeah, I see, I see what you're really about."

Look directly into their eyes and see where they actually look. Do they look back at you? Do they look to the side? Do they look down? There are so many things that are important to know that you only can experience if you're willing to get up close, get up real close.

When you have triggers, pull them close to you. It's going to feel awful. It's okay. You can handle it. You've been trained. Pull them close and don't think about what to do. The warrior doesn't think. The warrior trusts in the skills, the learning, and the practice he has done. You know how to move with your triggers; don't let fear keep you from them. Pull them close like a lover. They are your most intimate friends, after all. Your triggers have been with you longer than any partner. They are your most intimate companions, so pull them close. Pull them very close. Hold them there. Don't expect to know what to do with the triggers, allow the answer to be revealed to you.

The intensity of your triggers will diminish in size with the attention you pay to them. They must. For your high vibrational conscious exploration replaces the low vibrational habitual state of triggers. Don't fall for the idea that because you're uncomfortable something is necessarily wrong. Hold the position of, "Yeah, of course I'm uncomfortable. I'm contemplating something that's bothered me for 40 years. I'd be strange if I weren't."

Hold your triggers close. Watch them. Watch them dance in you. Watch them ask for your attention. Use all of your tools, but don't hide from the triggers. Don't let them slip away. Don't get distracted. Stand toe to toe with them.

When you're facing your triggers, if you start to waiver in your courage, just imagine that we stand behind you. We stand there to show you that you don't have to fear that you are not enough. You can be afraid of the triggers, but don't be afraid that you're not enough. You have a good team-mate and we have slaughtered so many fears. There's not yet one that has stood in front of us that has not gone down. We know what it's like to stand on the battlefield and be afraid. We know what it's like for you to face your trigger and allow yourself to still act, to still move. That's courage. We will stand beside you in consciousness and courage any time you wish.

Tools

Clarity vs. certainty

You are programmed in the fear-based operating system to look for certainty. Certainty says, "I'm not going to risk any change unless I know ahead of time how it's going to work out."

Certainty is a fallacy; it is actually impossible to be certain of anything, but the habit of seeking it runs very deep.

Clarity is the opportunity to experience insight. Clarity is only accessible in the moment. It does not come from the thinking mind, but is inspiration received by connecting with your soul's perspective.

Clarity is, "Oh, yeah, that's a good idea," without having any connection to the outcome of using that idea. Certainty is, "I will not act unless I know how it's going to turn out. I'm not going to leave this marriage, I'm not going to leave this job, I'm not going to move from this apartment, unless I know where the next man is going to come from, where the next job is going to be, and where the next house is going to be. I won't leave until I know. I won't change until I know. I can't make a difference in my life until I know how it's going to be." That's certainty. Clarity is, "This relationship doesn't work for me." See how it's just so much calmer? "This relationship doesn't work for me. I don't have to know what the next relationship is going to be in order to act on the fact that this one doesn't work anymore." That's clarity. And the beauty of clarity is, clarity leads to clarity. Certainty stops. Certainty is contracting. Clarity is expanding. Clarity says, "Here is insight." Certainty says, "Until I know, I'm not going to go".

It's so much more fun to live from clarity because it always opens, opens, opens. Certainty just closes doors. When you follow clarity, it opens up more opportunities; when you wait for certainty, you can wait a really long, miserable time. In fact, you'll wait forever.

At times, the cry for certainty can be very loud; however, it is quite fascinating to see how often you are willing to operate in clarity without realizing it.

Let's say you want to go to the park for a walk. You don't know who you're going to run into, but it doesn't forestall you from going for a walk. You don't know if you're going to be warm or cold, you don't know if you're going to have the right clothes to deal with the weather. It could start raining and you don't have a raincoat. That level of uncertainty you are okay with. "Wear layers, it'll work out. Bring an umbrella, don't bring an umbrella, who cares?" Yeah, you might run into somebody, you might not.

You can do all that and not have to contend with certainty's cry for attention. However, when you get into the relationship realms, "I don't know how she feels about me," "I don't know how he feels about me," "Is he going to want to stay married to me," "Is my kid going to do well in school today?" All of a sudden, certainty is back in charge.

Notice the temptation, return to the moment, ask for clarity.

***

Veronica writes:

This one took a while to sink in for me. I was confused about how to let go of certainty when clarity felt so elusive. However, when I finally realized that certainty was actually elusive and clarity was real, it really was quite a transformation.

***

My two favorite tools are "I don't know anything" and "clarity vs. certainty." These tools have helped me by turning off "mind chatter" and not needing to have security in all things and choosing clarity over certainty has helped. I am less concerned now about survival needs and requirements but feel for sure that clarity and potentials offer me a greater sense of freedom and peace vs. having to have security at all times before I act.

—J.R., Ontario, Canada

***

How often this comes up! Certainty now has a visceral "tag" for me. It feels tense, as if I'm boxed tightly all around my body when I'm trying to figure something out. I recall "clarity" and relax into a spacious listening posture. Clarity's point of reference is right now—open and available to anything new. Insight, seeing into the "clear bead at the center" wherein lies all possibility.

This makes "not know" a curious adventure instead of scary. I no longer expect myself to figure things out with my admittedly fine mind. I do expect that my mind will find the words to express what I gain from my insights and when I sense the authentic truth of my heart. A relaxed mind that observes my current reality has more access to intelligent and creative self-expression.

—Margy Henderson

Feet under shoulders

A quick way to ask yourself if you are coming from a balanced and centered place. "Are my feet under my shoulders?" A very important tool for those that are working to heal service mentality. Also powerful when you find yourself trying to convince someone you are right. Are you leaning forward to make your point or are you centered within yourself?

***

Veronica writes:

I love that this tool has such a strong visual component. It is quick to use and very easy to remember.

How ridiculous does it have it get?

How ridiculous does it have to get before you are willing to change a habit? How much suffering must you experience? How many times do you have to experience the same patterns?

How ridiculous does it have to get? The answer? Usually, pretty damned ridiculous.

You're constantly putting up barrier after barrier after barrier to taking responsibility for your creation because the habit of victimhood is so strong in you. Sure, the choice for consciousness is challenging, but suffering is painful and repetitive. Owning "I did this" might be hard, but what is the alternative?

Don't require it to become ridiculous before you are willing to transform it. If it has become ridiculous, then transform it immediately!

***

Veronica writes:

When it gets ridiculous, I KNOW whatever it is must move to the top of my to-do list. I must stop and become as conscious as possible about what is going on and what I am experiencing. When it is ridiculous, I bust out all the tools until it isn't ridiculous anymore!

***

I remember this tool when I notice things building to a frenzy and chaos begins to reign. It reminds me to get conscious quick—and often leads to a bout of laughter!

—Randy Sue Collins

***

How ridiculous does it have to get? This tool is actually somewhat soothing for me. Living in a foreign country with a busy schedule and acclimating to new standards and rules, many interesting and exasperating scenarios pop up daily. At one point, I was writing them all down because I didn't know what to do with them and all the emotional responses that were getting triggered. With this tool, I can be amused. I can laugh more. And it helps me focus on what I get to look at—on why this is happening FOR me, or what is the VELCRO here, who is answering the door, why this is in my lap—it is a personal inner adventure more than an external chronicle of events.

—Anna R., Mexico

I don't know anything

You really do not know ANYTHING, and this should please you. You don't know anything about this moment because you have never been in it before. You are brand-new here.

Your human life has been one of limitation. Spiritual growth is all about transformation and expansion. As you move along your spiritual journey, you move into brand-new territory, territory you truly don't know anything about.

You have the opportunity here to say, "I don't know anything. I only know about limitation and I'm not satisfied only knowing limitation. I am ready to live an expanded experience, and in order to do so I have to acknowledge I don't know a darn thing about living in an expanded way." Because you don't. You absolutely do not know a thing about living an expanded life.

What you're saying is, "I don't know anything about what's going on. I don't have an opinion about it. I don't have a judgment about it. I don't have any insight about it other than the insight I open up to."

The first step whenever you're trying to open up to a new possibility is to say, "I don't know anything in this moment about this." You've never been in this moment asking this question before. So, that's not a lie. That's not a crutch. That's not a coping mechanism. It is the truth. And truth immediately puts you into a higher-vibrational state, which makes accessing further insight easier and easier.

Stay open with: "I don't know anything about now, but I know what I bring to now." You don't come into the now as a babe fresh out of the womb. You come into the now with the collection of yourself, and the best you can do is to be in the now with an open and receptive position that allows you to evaluate and interact with the experience as it unfolds.

By saying "I don't know how to do it," or "I don't know anything about it," that becomes the truth, it clears the decks, it sort of starts you over. And it starts you over where? Right here. Not back to the beginning, but right here and now. So, "I don't know anything about it."

Immediately after "I don't know anything," comes "Am I bringing the past or the future into this moment?" That is your habit. "I don't know, but I have to look for an answer." Monitor yourself for the past creeping in to say, "It's never worked before, I've been trying so hard." Or the future popping up.

If the past and future shows up, return to "I don't know anything." Don't allow the habit of leaving the moment to run the show.

Let go of preconceived notions. Let go of future projections. Allow in the expansiveness that you have never ever experienced before. This is the good stuff.

And remember that there's a lot of fascination in every moment, especially when you don't decide you know what's going on. So "What is true now?" may get you into that peaceful state and then it's, "I don't know anything about this peaceful state," because you don't want to project old patterns into the truth of you. You want to explore the truth of you and being able to say "I don't know anything about this" helps keep you from bringing old baggage into that new moment.

When we first gave you the "I don't know anything" tool, we were met with a lot of resistance. The resistance came because you have big brains and you're super-smart, and when we said, "You don't know anything," you all went: "Arrgghh! Yes, I do know something."

Eventually, the response changed to: "Wow, that's the biggest help I've ever had—to not have to always feel like I'm on the hook to know everything."

***

Veronica writes:

Oh, this one made people MAD! I got so many emails saying, "What do they mean, I don't know anything?!" Probably because I was saying the same thing to myself! We are so accustomed to being judged by our knowledge. When this tool clicked for me, it was a gate latch that sounded like a sonic boom. You mean, I don't HAVE to know everything to feel safe? You mean, I can just be? A revolutionary idea.

***

My ego did not like this tool at first, but using it over and over let me off the hook of needing an answer for anything. Ego out of the way lets Soul's perspective come through.

—Randy Sue Collins

***

"I don't know anything" clearly shows me how I make assumptions and draw conclusions on subjects of which I have no knowledge.

—Mike

***

My favorite tool, "I don't know anything," is subtle yet intensely profound. When its meaning is truly grasped there is great comfort in knowing you really don't know anything. Ironically, this may not be a popular concept in spiritual circles as many aspirants I've come across think they "know everything."

—John M.

Lay it down and walk away

When you release something from your life or your energetic field, be sure that you release it completely; lay it down and walk away from it.

We see a lot of things in your energy field that are old and unneeded, but there is a sense of: "It's served me for so long I should hang onto it." It's kind of like the junk drawer in your house or those mismatched socks that you just can't bear to part with. There is an energy that says, "I might need this someday," and on a stuff level that could be true, but when you are dealing with energetics it's debilitating. It really is. In order to carry around that energetic, you have to also carry around the vibration of that energetic. If the vibration of that energetic oscillates, literally oscillates at a lower rate than the rest of you, it sets up an interference pattern. This gets in the way of you raising your vibration and it blocks you from becoming more conscious.

The conscious act is to lay it down and walk away. "What am I willing to lay down; from what am I willing to walk away? What am I willing to actually completely abandon? To fully and completely let go? What am I willing to lay down?"

It is not enough anymore to say: "I just want to release this." We're going to change the language. "Can I lay it down and walk away?" If you never, ever again access that memory, if you never, ever again did that habit, if you never, ever again ate that food, can you be comfortable with that? What we suspect you'll find is that with some of these you think they're gone, you think you've let them go, you think you've released them, you think you've dropped them, but they're just sort of in your wake. They are caught up in you and they follow you around. You have an extraordinary amount of this stuff in your fields and it's absolutely and completely the time to make the commitment to lay it down and walk away from it. There can be dependencies, co-dependencies. There can be addictions—addictions to people, addictions to energy, addictions to things. The idea is "I don't need this in my life. It has served me, it has shown me, it has taught me, but I'm ready to move into something else to learn from and I'm willing to lay it down and walk away from it."

Don't fall for the trap of thinking that means you're littering energetically or anything silly like that. It doesn't work that way.

Now, this may bring up your abandonment issues because you're abandoning something that's been part of you. It doesn't matter if this thing has served you or not, if it's helped you or not, if it's even been positive or not, it will bring up some of your abandonment issues to leave it, to lay it down and walk away. When you get that feeling of: "Wow, I feel like I'm abandoning it," you can say, "What is it about this thing that's still got its hooks in me? Why has it still got a hold of me? What is it that I think somehow I owe to it?" Sometimes these bad habits have become like friends to you. Your friendship has not been a very positive friendship, but it's still a friendship nonetheless.

If the truth is that it does not serve you, if the truth is that it's not helping you grow, if the truth is that it's not revealing the highest version of you, if the truth is that it's not helping you see the next version of you that you wish to experience, it may be time to lay it down and walk away from it. If you feel abandonment when making those choices, ask yourself, "Am I a victim of my choices? Do I feel victimized by the choices I'm making?"

When you are done, be done all the way. Lay it down and walk away from it.

***

Veronica writes:

I have found that "laying it down and walking away" often requires multiple attempts. Or, more accurately, it requires that I am very specific about what I am "laying down." As an example, I can lay down a relationship, but then it pops up again! I've learned to lay down specific aspects of the relationship as they arrive. This has really helped me apply this tool.

***

This can be a hard tool for me since I am used to operating from my "pack rat" mentality, from my habitual place of fear and wanting to manage everything around me for that elusive feeling of safety, I want to hang onto everything whether it serves me or not. By remembering to lay it down and walk away, I can clear away baggage that's been holding me back for years. I don't want the clutter anymore, in my house or in myself!

—*Randy Sue Collins*

***

This is a very useful tool for dealing with my "nagging" baggage and habits. It allows me to instantly become centered in the NOW. It helps me stay focused and on course.

—*Mike*

***

I've been using this tool a lot lately. It seems to be universal in its application. If I find myself tempted to go into fear, I isolate the problem and then "lay it down and walk away." I then often ask the Guardians for help in clearing my field of any lingering detritus. And, yes, whatever the problem, it often needs to be addressed more than once because of the nuanced layers of fear, resistance, baggage that need to be released. I also use this tool when I become aware of attachments: habits, usually, that no longer serve me. Then there is the uncertainty factor. If I become aware of trying to control a situation, I lay that down and walk away, too, so that I can move into clarity and the circle of possibilities. All in all, a very usable and useful tool to keep close at hand.

—*Janice*

Mad scientist

If you are in a situation that you are unhappy with, rather than leave the situation, experiment within the situation. Let's say you are in a job you do not like. Rather than find a new job, consider staying in the present situation but approaching it in a brand new way.

Then when you start to make changes, you're the only thing that is changing. This makes it much easier for you to see the dynamic play out.

Become the mad scientist and start experimenting, and by experimenting we mean changing what you think the outcome of *you* being in *your* integrity is. You think you can't be in your integrity because you'll get fired or because they won't like you or because, because, because. You have all these projections, all these fears about what being in your integrity means. Change your energetic and see how it plays out. You don't like where you are now so it's worth taking a chance that it could get better, and you will learn a lot about yourself in the process. Make what you are not happy with your little factory for experimentation.

Show up at work, sit down, and instead of saying, "God, look at all this work, look at all these voicemails, and oh, the boss is already bitching at me," try this, "OK, I'm a mad scientist today and this is my factory. What do I want to create? How do I want to be in this space? I don't mind the work. I mind the attitudes. So, how are those attitudes true about me? How is my bitchy boss just a voice in my head that's really loud when it comes out of somebody else's mouth?" You are able to look at things in a new way because you are not requiring the situation stay the same in order for you to feel safe. You use the process of experimentation to create a reality with less suffering and more self-awareness.

Experiment!

***

Veronica writes:

I love the mad scientist tool. It's nice to have such permission to experiment in a difficult situation. Oftentimes, a painful dynamic is really just a specific thing or person and there is actually a lot more about the situation that I like than I don't like. The mad scientist tool lets me keep the parts I enjoy while I attempt to transform the parts I don't. It can be a lot of fun!

***

This is a fun tool. When I become a mad scientist I really see how different a situation can become just by my changing the perception of it. That's really all it takes. It's amazing how quickly a trigger can get diffused by using the mad scientist tool.

—Randy Sue Collins

***

We think of a mad scientist as trying many different combinations of things to come up with the magic jackpot. When there is a problem, I look first at what I can do—which usually hasn't worked—then I think, "A mad scientist would try many different approaches to try and solve the issue."

An example jumps to my mind. I returned my phone equipment as instructed to a local UPS store. This took about 40 minutes even though there were only two people ahead of me. Since I had so much time and I was practicing being sincerely in the moment, I heard and retained the stories and intentions of the customers ahead of me. I knew where their packages were going and what they were shipping. When it came to my turn, all went smoothly. The service person apologized for the wait. I remained in the moment and happy.

Upon returning to my car, I jotted a note in my date book that I had sent the package and that I had a receipt. Weeks later I received a notice from the phone company that I was being charged $150 on my credit card because I didn't return the equipment on time. I searched for my paperwork. I had part of it, but no receipt. I looked and looked everywhere, old receipt files, new ones, high and low, every place I might have put it, and it was nowhere to be found.

Then I thought, "Maybe I didn't get one." I looked at my datebook and confirmed that I did get a receipt. I checked in with the mad scientist, "How else can I prove this, what else can I do?" I remembered the details about the other people and the time of their transactions. I got excited that being in the moment had rewarded me with the knowledge of where UPS would have record of my transaction. Just then I looked down at a bag tucked behind the couch and went, "Whoa!" A quick look inside revealed my original receipt.

Problem resolved. This tool reminds us there are many ways to look at and solve problems. It reminds me to try everything I can think of.

—Rosie

Neutral observation

A tool that says, "I'm not going to take my habitual response as the mandated action." It means, "I'm going to stop and ask what is actually going on here in this moment."

Neutral observation is like carving out a little space that says, "In this moment, instead of all the habitual ways I could react, I'm going to open to hearing a new way, open to insight from my soul, and ask, 'What is this teaching me?' and, 'What am I learning?' to carve out a space where my reaction can be something new rather than habitual."

Neutrality doesn't have duality in it. Neutrality doesn't have judgments in it. Neutrality doesn't have all these places within you that you have habitually gone with situations. That's one of the reasons that it's hard to go into neutral observation, because you have all these little niches in you where your habits runs. Habit takes you here, habit takes you there, and you're just thinking, "How can I be neutral in this moment?" Well, it takes a little practice. You're literally rewiring your neural pathways in order for this to work.

So, let's say you have insecurity about a project, "Oh, I have this project and I don't know how it's going to turn out." If you're in the fear, then it's "I don't know what's going to happen," and you start hamster-wheel thinking, "I should do this, maybe I should do this, maybe I shouldn't have started this." Everybody knows what that feels like. If we take that up into a higher-vibration space, it's "Wow, there's that feeling in my chest again, interesting, it's showing up again. There's that feeling of 'there's potential for failure here.' Wow, failure is a judgment. The truth is, everything's a learning experience. If I can look at this neutrally, then the outcome isn't what drives this experience. This fear is based on a need for a certain outcome. These feelings in my body are being elicited by a need for a certain outcome. If I can see this neutrally and just say 'Wow, there's that fear, there's that habit popping up again, I can feel it in my chest, I see it in my life, but I'm not attached to the outcome that that fear is trying to get me to attach to'."

The fear is saying, "The shit's hitting the fan." Neutral observation says, "Everything's interesting." When you can stay neutral, you can feel the fear but say, "I'm just going to see it. I'm not going to let the feeling of the fear tell me what to do next, I'm going to let neutral observation and insight from my soul reveal what's going to happen next, and every time that fear stirs up in me, I'm going to make another choice for insight. I'm going to make another choice just to watch it rather than let it drive the experience I'm in." And that, of course, takes a little bit of practice but those neural pathways will lay down very quickly because it's a high-vibrational activity and because it actually leads to so much relief of the body's tension.

When you can sit in neutral observation and say, "I see the body reacting but that's not the choice I'm making", the body starts to calm. You "calm" into a higher vibration rather than "stir up" in a lower vibration. And that's really the cusp of this whole thing. Watch the fear, knowing it's an option and not a mandate. Choose again and again to see it, rather than be it. Even if you feel it, still say, "I see you, fear. I feel you trying to show up in my life and run the show but I'm not going on that path. I'm not attached to the outcome you're trying to scare me about. I'm going to sit here and I'm going to be as neutral as possible and point you out to myself," and the fears will dissipate. They have to. Because when you take something that's low-vibration and infuse it with high-vibration, it can't last. It's like putting an ice cube in a microwave. It can't last. Biologically incompatible. It can't last in that environment.

Neutral observation is not numb. Neutral observation is being extremely aware of what is going on and choosing to have as neutral as possible experience of it.

Neutral observation doesn't make you a doormat. In fact, neutral observation only works when you set boundaries.

***

Eloheim: Neutral observation stops in the moment, collects what the moment is offering, sets boundaries, and then moves into, "Where's the aha, where's the learning, where's the next step here?" and then into action, which leads to a new moment, which leads to an opportunity for neutral observation.

Response: Which is so hard.

Eloheim: We understand. But we also see very clearly that when you live in habitual response, it's painful. Neutral observation is challenging but habitual response is painful.

Response: Where's the switch to turn it on and off?

Eloheim: It's really spiritual choice. It's that choice that says, "I know I'm in habit. I know I'm in a coping mechanism. I know I'm using fear. I know I'm bringing the past or the future into this moment." It's just catching yourself and then saying to yourself, "I know where this leads." It's like when you have a bad breakup and you're listening to a sad song on the radio and you have your hand on the phone and you're gonna call. You're gonna call that person that just broke up with you and you know, you have your hand on the phone and you know, what's going to happen when you dial that phone. You know it's going to be ugly. You know they don't want to hear from you. You know that you're going to hear stuff that you don't want to hear; even if you get the answering machine, you don't want to hear the answering machine, you don't even know what you want from the person, you just know that that's what you think is your coping mechanism. That pain on the other side of the phone.

Now, to let go of the phone, to be conscious—to sit with that is very challenging and it can be emotional, but you know what happens if you pick up the phone, so you have a choice. And the choice is to be disciplined enough to say that the habit of picking up the phone is less attractive than the challenge of becoming conscious in this moment.

Neutral observation doesn't mean numb. Neutral observation means, "I don't know everything, therefore I'm going to open to my soul helping me see all that I can so that I choose, state preferences, and set boundaries in order to operate from the most grace, ease, and bliss possible in this dynamic." And that can be applied to every single moment.

***

Veronica writes:

Oh yes, Neutral observation, my old friend. This was one of the first tools Eloheim ever gave us. It feels like putting on a comfortable pair of jeans or my favorite boots. Relaxing into an alternative to the hamster-wheel mind and the requirement to know everything.

***

To me, Neutral observation is one of the most important and useful tools of all. When I am in neutral observation, I immediately go into the present moment and I become aware, at a gut level, that my thinking mind holds a gentle tyranny over me. If I'm not very aware, it runs my life through habitual patterns and knee-jerk reactions. This practice has also made me aware that there is room for very little or no spontaneous action on my part when the habitual mind is in control. I live much more cleanly and peacefully when I can remember to stay in Neutral observation.

    —Janice Imbach

***

This tool helps me step back and not take things so damn seriously. Allows the bigger picture to be seen.

    —Randy Sue Collins

***

Neutral observation stops me from becoming overly emotional when I am triggered. I find myself in a space where time seems to stand still and provides an opportunity for me to view my situation and its many options.

    —Donna Price

"No" is a complete sentence / Say "no" first

This tool allows you to set a boundary or state a preference without feeling the need to justify or make excuses for your position. You are not responsible for others' reactions to your choices. Stating a preference is an act of free will.

A fascinating way to learn about boundaries, preferences, and "What is true now?" is to say "no" first. Just give it a try! Someone calls you up and asks you to go out. Say "no" first.

If you are habitually saying "yes" to keep other people happy, try saying "no" and seeing how it makes you feel. The result we have seen is that being able to just say no is incredibly liberating. Importantly, it gives you the time to actually find out how you feel. When you say no first, you can then consider your feelings on the matter without the pressure of having the question hanging over your head.

If you decide that you actually do want to participate——because YOU want to, not just to make another happy—you can always call back and say you changed your mind.

And "No, period" is a complete sentence. You don't have to explain. There is no need for a lie, an excuse, or even other plans. If you are asked, "Why?" you can just say, "It's just not right for me."

If they don't respect that, well, that is something very good to know about them, isn't it?

***

Veronica writes:

Oh yeah, NO… who knew? When I started saying NO first and then giving myself time to check in about how I felt, my life changed. What else is there to add?

Point fingers

You can't point fingers anymore, meaning you no longer have the option of saying that someone else or something else creates in your life. Nothing else can create in your life, and every time you point your finger and decide how it's going to be, and decide and decide and decide, you're turning over the only power you have in this life, which is the power to create your reality using your free will. You can go right along living the victim mentality quite nicely, but if you actually want to experience the magnificence that's possible with the Homo sapiens moving into Homo spiritus paradigm you have to stop looking at other people and other things as creating in your reality and start to recognize and acknowledge that you are the one. You are the one who put it there.

It can be hard when you realize, "Oh my God, I point fingers every second of every day." However, this realization allows you to access the wow of responsibility, the wow of creatorship, the wow of: "Yes, I did that. Yes, I did that. I did it for me. I did it for me so that I could have the experience that that scenario offers me."

The idea that you can't point fingers at anybody anymore is a radical concept. It says, "Everybody in my life, everything in my life, is my creation. And as my creation I take 100 percent responsibility for it being there and I take 100 percent responsibility for how I choose to interact with it." When you stop pointing fingers, it's not: "Why the hell is this in my life?" It's: "Wow, *this* is in my life!" And that's a big shift. That's a big shift. It was a big shift to get into 100 percent responsibility, even if taking 100 percent responsibility meant "I'm taking responsibility even though I don't like it."

Now it's: "I'm taking responsibility, I know there's something here for me, I don't have to figure it out as much as I have to allow myself to experience it without throwing barrier after barrier after barrier up between me and the experience."

***

Veronica writes:

I remember quite clearly the night that The Council talked with us about no more pointing fingers. I was struck with the power of this idea. It really is quite a shift to go from seeing yourself as a victim to realizing you are a creator. Then, to start realizing that you created everything (even the shitty bits!), well, that's a doozy. To further realize that you can't pin it on anyone else, even when they "did" it… it's a lot of responsibility. However, it's my responsibility to work with my creations and my reactions to them. This puts the ball in my court, which suits me just fine.

***

The part I remember about "pointing fingers" is that when I point my finger at someone else, one finger is pointing away from me and the other three fingers are pointing back at me. Just a little reminder that I created this situation to show me something about myself. I created it to have a learning experience, which is liberating. Taking responsibility for my creations instead of spinning and suffering in victimhood is quite a relief.

—Mary T

***

It is really easy to point fingers at any person and say "This is happening because you did this." That is pointing fingers at someone else instead of saying that I have created this to learn from it. I am taking the power of creating what happens to (for) me instead of simply going along for the ride. It gives a person a sense of confidence that you have a hand in what is going on.

—Rosie

Preferences/Judgments

Judgment is not the same as preference. Judgment is the belief that you have to have a position *against* something in order to have a position *preferring* something. So, all of a sudden the choice between chocolate and vanilla must become, "Chocolate is a good flavor and vanilla is a bad flavor, so I am going with chocolate because that's the good flavor," instead of just saying, "I have a preference for chocolate."

You're an immortal, infinite soul that chooses to have every experience you can manage. If you set out a lot of judgments and you start saying that vanilla's wrong, then when it comes around time to experience vanilla you have to deal with the baggage of already assigning it as "wrong." It's always nice to not put extra baggage on things that you'll probably get around to wanting to experience someday. It's also quite helpful to limit the amount of baggage (static) about anything you are experiencing.

Most of the time, we see that you had to make one thing wrong—sometimes VERY wrong—in order to set a preference because you weren't feeling strong enough to just say "No" is a complete sentence.

When you are new to boundaries and preferences you will sometimes believe that you have to get really worked up in order to use them. Actually, when you discover "What is true now?," you can set boundaries and state preferences from a very calm place.

Keep in mind that there is a damned good reason for having a preference, which is: You're a soul experiencing the physical form in a free-will zone. So, if you don't have some preferences, what the heck is the point of being here in the first place? Not very much that we can see. Having preferences is the one of the main events!

Someone once said to us, "Well, if we are infinite and immortal, aren't we going to do everything?" And we said yes, but you do them in an order. There's an order to it. In a linear sense, there's an order to it. Where today you decided to eat chocolate, tomorrow you're going to decide to eat vanilla. So, even if you're immortal and infinite, you're still deciding right now to be here instead of being someplace else. Preference. Choice. Free will. You don't need to have something be wrong in order to have something else be what you want to do.

Coming from judgment is low-vibrational. It takes a lot of energy to stay invested in a judgment. It can be difficult to change your mind because you are so invested energetically in the judgment. Sometimes your identity can even be wrapped up in a judgment, which makes it that much harder to change. Judgments don't serve you, on so many levels.

***

Veronica writes:

Another tool to help you realize that you get to choose. This one helps me clarifies when I am actually choosing and when I am running an unconscious habit, which shows up as a judgment. I like vanilla and chocolate ice cream so this example is perfect for me. It really is expressing a preference in the moment rather than deciding on a right/wrong.

***

This tool has whittled down my list of people, situations, and things that I have judgments around and helps me realize how many judgments came through societal conditioning. Preferences allow for choice through fascination and true passion of my life's purpose. It brings me closer to the relaxed feeling of contentment and fulfillment.

—Deb

Script holding/Script-holders

You are the only thing that is going on. Everything else—all of the physical structures you see, the plants, the animals, the people, the houses, you name it—all things in your life are just actors in *your* play.

They act in your play in order to give you opportunities to grow. We call them script-holders. Imagine that everyone is walking around carrying a really, really big script. When you do something—you respond to a trigger, repeat a habit, feel fear, act consciously—all the actors in your play are then give a cue to turn to a certain page in your script.

As an example, a guy pulls in front of you on the freeway. This triggers you into a habitual and unconscious revisiting of other experiences when you felt like you weren't seen. You then start to relive the pain of those past experiences. You are completely disconnected from the moment you are in. Your choice to be unconscious directs the driver to turn to page 500 and it instructs him to flip you off. This is likely to further upset you and may result in additional unpleasant interactions with the driver.

If your response was, "Wow, check that out, that guy just pulled in front of me. I'm going to stay in the moment with my reaction. I'm going to be conscious about what comes up for me. I'm going to recognize the temptation to go into the past, but I'm committed to staying with how I actually feel right now." The next thing you know, the driver has sped away and he's gone out of your life. Your choice to respond consciously directed him to turn to page 750 which says: "Just speed away. You've done your part."

As you become more conscious and you start directing your play—creating your reality is another way to say it—then you have people turning to the pages in the script where they respond to your emanation of consciousness. You make conscious choices, you emanate consciousness, and they turn to the pages that are all about consciousness. This is how your emanation moves out into the world and affects your manifestations. In effect, you're telling all your script-holders to reflect the consciousness you're emanating. If you do encounter script holders that react in an unconscious manner, you set a boundary by saying, "Oh no, no, I'm on page 500 because it's my job to reflect consciousness back even though you're giving me unconsciousness."

Your perspective shifts to, "Everything in my play is my responsibility and my creation," because you're putting it there through your choices. Your choices of what to think, how to handle habits, how to manage triggers, how to process interactions you have with people, how to deal with the temptation to live in the past or the future. "What's the next act going to be? Well, the next act is going to be an act of consciousness and I'm going to emanate consciousness into the world so that everyone around me has the opportunity to turn to a new page."

Another way to say this is: Your internal world generates your external experience. That's why you can change internally, never speak a word to the other person, and the dynamic between you can shift. Why? Because you're saying: "I want page 500 out of you instead of page 300." Energetically you are emanating a different connection to them and they are responding with a different response, turning to a different page.

You will find it fascinating to view your world as full of script holders. We love to hear stories like, "I know that guy's script-holding for me because he just said the exact words that my mom used to say to me and he has on the same shirt that my dad used to wear! God, talk about good script-holding."

There is one aspect of script-holding that we want you to be very, very clear about. Let's say you have a little tête à tête with somebody—you don't get to say, "Well, I must be holding script for you." No. It doesn't work that way. No, no, no. That's missing the point. If you have a little tête à tête—stay in you. What is it that you're experiencing about their interaction with you? It's not, "This is awkward so I must be holding script for *you*." It's, "This is awkward and you are holding script for me to see what I can learn here."

Recognize the truth that you're all here to facilitate each other's growth. In all interactions that you're experiencing, look around, see the other parties as actors in your play, and recognize how they are acting is affecting your growth and your journey. When you can see other people as actors in your play, it can oftentimes take away the intensity or the trigger of the dynamic, and instead help you to see what's going on as neutrally as possible.

Another important aspect of script-holding is this: Everyone is an actor in your play and you're an actor in everyone else's play. It's all happening at the same time. You are having simultaneous experiences of being the script-holder and the center of the play. This is a great thing! There's room for everybody to be center-stage *and* for everyone to be a script holder as well. It's beautiful.

You've all agreed to participate in this dynamic with each other. It's really cool. You've all said: "Hey, let's play make-believe. Let's play make-believe; I'll help you and you help me."

***

Veronica writes:

It's very powerful to see the world as "holding script" for you. I find it especially helpful to do this when I am strongly triggered by something. It puts a bit of distance between the event and my emotional state, which helps me get a new perspective.

***

I use this tool all the time and also find myself reminding my teens to use it, too. Knowing that I assigned everyone in my play (my life) helps to remind me that I truly am the creator of my experiences. It's a great way to feel empowered immediately.

—Randy Sue Collins

***

I know that script holders are a direct reflection of me. When someone causes me discomfort, I thank them for showing me a habit or baggage that must be dealt with. It works quickly and dramatically changes the dynamics of the situation.

—Mike

***

Someone called me a bully yesterday (which I still am finding fascinating...). He could have said nothing, since I wasn't even talking to him or he could have said that the person I was verbally sparring with had a weaker argu-ment—compounded by the fact that he was louder, upset, and wouldn't stop defending his position—but no, he told me very clearly to stop bullying my classmate. I had been playfully telling the vice-president of the class that it was his obligation to let all of us know about the free tickets the school was giving away to the soccer game this weekend (of which he scored 4)...mind you, I already had plans for Friday night. Bully? How ridiculous does it have to get? This guy was really holding script for me. I can't control what other people think of me. I can't control others' projections onto me. Do I not say anything anymore? That would turn me to a page I know I don't need to go to again. I'll just thank this guy for helping me move on in my algorithm of consciousness.

—Anna R.

Strongest chakra

Look at your chakras and identify which ones you're really strong in and which chakras you tend to ignore. Once you have a sense of this, try this experiment: Rather than default to behaving from your strongest chakra, see what it's like to interact with the world from your less-developed chakras.

As an example, for some people it's easy to talk about a subject (5th chakra), but it's harder to be open hearted about it (4th chakra.) For other people it's really easy to power through things (3rd chakra), but they can't see the mystical sides of a subject easily (7th chakra). Perhaps they are very sexual (2nd chakra), but don't see things clearly (6th chakra).

It's not wrong to be weaker in a certain chakra; it's just like a muscle that you haven't worked on. Ideally, you are balanced in all of your chakras and can operate from any of them.

Another way to use the strongest chakra tool is in relationships. When you're interacting with someone, especially someone you care about, someone you want to be closer to, you can make things more comfortable for them by interacting with them from their strongest chakra. This may mean that you abide in a more uncomfortable state than you are accustomed to. However, since you want to balance your chakras, this is great practice!

It's typically pretty easy to determine which one or two chakras that a person is strongest in. Once you have a sense of this, interact with them from that chakra. Do they like to talk? Then talk with them. Are they "touchy feely"? Then be more physical with them. Are they very powerful? Then be powerful, too.

They are an expert in their most powerful chakra. Interact with them from their strongest chakra and you will learn how to be an expert in that chakra as well.

It's important to note that few people operate from their first chakra as their strongest chakra. The first chakra is the connection to safety and security. To feel powerful in this chakra, you will need to create a new relationship to fears and the survival instinct. Is it surprising that these are the very issues we talk about with you?

***

Veronica writes:

YIKES! There, I said it! This tool can be such a challenge. I'm 5ᵗʰ chakra dominate. Lately I've been working on opening my heart chakra. Turns out that talking about heart opening isn't really how you do that. Talk about setting aside a strength in order to build a different strength! However challenging, getting in touch with my heart chakra has been a stunning process and well worth the journey. Which one will I focus on next?!

***

When I remember this tool, I find that I always am leading with my throat chakra when communicating with others, and can run over anyone with my words. This tool reminds me to back off from using my loudest and strongest chakra and relax into communicating from my other chakras. The result is a more meaningful exchange with whomever I'm with. It allows the other person the safe space to be themselves too, without the fear of me dominating them.

—Randy Sue Collins

Vulnerability vs. weakness

Weakness is when you're in a position where you don't feel secure, you don't feel strong, you don't have certainty, you don't feel completely safe, and you try to hide it or you lie about it. Vulnerability is when you're in the exact same position and you tell your truth about it. When you're in a position of vulnerability it's actually the ultimate strength because there's nothing hidden, you're not pretending, there's nothing fake, there is no way to topple you. You may crumble but you can't be toppled. You may crumble because you feel like, "Oh my God, this is the hardest thing I've ever had to deal with." Yeah, OK. You kind of crumble and then you use some tools and you perk yourself back up. But you don't get knocked off your center. Telling your truth keeps you centered.

Weakness is very low-vibrational because you are hiding the truth of you. Vulnerability is a high-vibrational position; your strength is revealed when you're willing to tell your truth. Weakness is very concerned about other people's actions: "What do they think? How will they react? How can I avoid them being upset with me?" Vulnerability doesn't require action from other people. Vulnerability says, "This is my truth." From that position, it is much easier to set clear and healthy boundaries.

An example: You're in a relationship and you feel you've fallen in love and you want to tell the person you've fallen in love with them. That's a big moment, right? Weakness would be: "God, I'm in love with this person but what if they don't love me back? How's it going to affect me? Oh God, oh God, oh God." Vulnerability is: "The truth is the truth and I'm in love with this person." Weakness would be: "I really respect this person, I enjoy their company, I like spending time with them, and I want to tell them that, but how are they going to receive that or then maybe once they know I like them so much they'll use that to manipulate my feelings or manipulate my actions or try to get stuff out of me." Vulnerability is: "I really like your company and I can still set boundaries even if I admit that. I like your company and if you start acting like an idiot I'm not going to like your company anymore and I'm going to move on from there."

If the word "vulnerability" is very triggering, you can use the word "open" or "openness." But we would encourage you to stick with "vulnerability." We use the word vulnerability because it's been misused for so long and we want to reclaim it. Most of the misused words we give up on, but this one we want to reclaim. The energy of vulnerability is so much like the rose opening. It's so much like the butterfly coming out of the cocoon. It's so much that point of: "Anything could happen." And what you most often think is: "Anything bad could happen." But in vulnerability there's: "Anything could happen, period."

***

Veronica writes:

A lot of the Council's tools are intellectual; this one is very emotional. For me, there is an intense feeling associated with being vulnerable and strong at the same time. Truth and openness can be strong? What a relief!

***

I learned from Eloheim that if I am living and expressing the truth of me, there is nothing to fear. Weakness seems fearful, like I'm being a victim; being vulnerable feels courageous. If it's the truth, then I can wear it proudly and come what may, I'm true to myself. I don't have to waste my time or energy trying to cover up, keep myself safe, hide, or tweak anything about my truth. I may be vulnerable because I am more exposed, but what is the point of riding a roller coaster gripping the sidebar, eyes clenched shut, huddled in a ball?

—Anna

***

I use this tool strategically to get from war to peace. I know that by relaxing into vulnerability I will win, and that is not weak!

—Denise

What is true now?

Asking yourself "What is true now?" is a way of staying connected to the moment and your soul's insight about the moment.

It's fairly easy to remember to say "What is true now," but it's also very easy to be habitual about the answer you allow yourself to experience. What is true now is not answered by the mind. What is true now is answered by an "aha" from the soul, so by asking yourself what is true now constantly, you're creating a very strong connection between you and your soul, which is a fine thing to do if you're interested in transforming your life. The truth of you must be experienced consciously.

If what is true now is answered by a sentence of, say, more than say 10 words, it's your mind. An "aha" from the soul is going to be shorter than that. It doesn't need to be lengthy because it's not processed by the mind. It's an energetic truth expressed briefly in order to really sink in. If what is true now starts to have a lengthy explanation, suspect that the mind is encroaching on the soul's turf and ask the mind to shut up.

When used with consistency and consciousness, what is true now can be used to uncover unconscious coping mechanisms and lies that you tell yourself.

***

Veronica writes:

Another tool to keep very close to you. I use this one a lot to help sort out when I am acting from my current preferences and when I am acting habitually or out of patterns from the past.

***

I like "what is true now." I find the greatest challenge is being aware when the chatter-y monkey-mind starts with its unsuspectingly clever maneuvering to make me feel uncomfortable or irritated or going around and around on the same conversation. Old news, stuff that is past its expiry date, as they say. When I realize it, I immediately go to "what is true now." What is usually "true now" is that I was enjoying whatever I was doing before the sneaky bits got into my conscious thoughts. It seems never-ending.

—Rosie

What's in your lap?

When you are tempted to get into somebody else's business or find yourself judging people and/or events, ask yourself "What's in my lap? What is going on in me? How does this reflect something in me?" You can't tell anybody else what they need to see or what they are seeing; you need to deal with what's in your lap.

Are you in this moment? What static are you aware of? Where are you lying to yourself? What are you afraid of?

Need we go on? There is PLENTY for you to focus on right there in your lap.

***

Veronica writes:

I love this, "Need we go on?" Eloheim specifically told me to put that in there.

***

I use this tool a lot when I'm triggered by my birth family. We have a lot of issues around lack that we've been working out with each other from the time we were children. So now, when one of my siblings calls to complain about not having enough money, I look at what it brings up in me, what's in my lap, and it helps me to not go into "savior" mode. When I am conscious about this, it amazes me how much the conversation can change.

—*Claire*

Where am I lying to myself?

What things do you have a hard time admitting to yourself? What are the things you don't want anyone else to know? What are the things you have kept hidden?

In order to realize your authentic expression, you can't be lying to yourself. "Where are the holdout places where I'm telling myself stories about who I am?" They're typically going to be around one of these areas: sex, money, relationships, job, health, and housing.

"Where am I lying to myself about my marriage?" The word lying is such a triggering word but we are using it on purpose, because in essence you're lying to yourself if you know your marriage isn't working for you and you don't say that to yourself. Don't fall into the belief that you have to act on this awareness, simply allow yourself to be conscious of what your truth is. This one step is powerfully transformative.

What is the truth that you haven't told yourself or you've hidden from other people? What's the thing you're embarrassed people will know about you? What is the thing you're trying not to think about all the time? "What is true now?" reveals the things that *can serve you*, "Where am I lying to myself?" reveals the things that you wish *you could ignore*. Where you lie to yourself generates static in your life.

***

Veronica writes:

At first, I thought this was going to be the same as What is true now?, but it is quite different. What is true now? helps me come back to the moment. Where am I lying to myself? helps me see why I don't want to be in the moment in the first place. Make sure to be nice to yourself when you discover where you are lying to yourself. It is easy to slip into judgment.

"Wow!", not "why?"

When you look at your creations, you typically say, "Why is this here?" This is not the question to ask. It is not: "Why is this here?" It's: "Wow, this is here. Wow, I am an amazing creator. Wow, I have generated something really, really complex, complicated, fascinating," whatever word you like, whatever word applies. But it's not: "Why?" It's: "Wow!" You have to shift out of the idea that you have to understand why it's here and instead say: "It is here."

An example is this: When you go to Disneyland and you ride around on the rides, you don't say, "Why are there pirates in the Pirates of the Caribbean?" You say, "Wow, I am transported into a completely new world here. What does this give me? What does this generate in me? What feelings am I having? Am I a little scared? Is it a little shocking? Is it a little surprising? Is it a little funny? Am I getting wet? Am I cold? What am I doing here? What is the experience I'm having in this wow?" You might get a bit brainiac and say, "Why did they choose that color paint?" or something like that, but don't take the example so far that it ruins it. Stay with the truth of it, which is when you find yourself in an experience it's not: "Why is this here?" It's: "Wow, look at my creation. And I'm going to acknowledge my creation."

You know you'll go to a movie theater and watch a very complex movie that's been created for you for your entertainment but you don't experience your own creations from that perspective. Like, "Wow, look at this fabulously detailed creation I have presented for myself, that I can explore, that I can roll around in, that I can feel wow about." So we'd like you to start experiencing your creations from that perspective where instead of a "why" you let yourself have a "wow." And that doesn't mean that it's not painful, but what it means is that when you're in it, you're not feeling pain because you feel like you're a victim, you're not feeling pain because you feel like you have no choices, you're not feeling pain because you feel stepped on. What you're feeling is: "Wow, this is just mind-blowing. This is just mind-blowing how detailed and in-depth and powerful it is that I've created this environment to explore. This is here for me to grow from. This is here for me to have an experience with and it's amazing."

***

Veronica writes:

Such a good reminder and such an easy one to remember! When I find myself saying, "Why?" I can just change it to "Wow!" What a shift of energy! It puts the focus on the fact that I created this and takes it off of the temptation to feel like I am a victim of my creation.

***

Since I'm a brainiac who comes from a long line of brainiacs, "Why?" has been my default method of operation. Breaking the victim habit hasn't been easy, but Wow! is a quick link to, "This is my awesome creation." It shifts the energy from dark and dank to light and cheery where insight is possible. Ha, I see the light!

—Mary T

***

When I get stuck in the repetitive circle of, "Why?" I don't feel good and realize that I am spinning my wheels in victimhood. When I say, "Wow... I created this," I feel more empowered and open to insight. I can feel my energy lift from "poor me" to "powerful me."

—Paula T

***

This tool changes my perspective on a dime. Often when a shift happens, I want to go into "Why?" "Why didn't he hear me?" "Why did she respond to me in that way?" and this can lead me into a big waste of time in which I am trying to figure out what part I have in other folks' responses to me. Other times, my "Why's" leads me into interminable ruminations of cause and effect that keep me in my head and out of the moment. The result is fatigue and low vibration and a perpetuated belief that I have control. Wow! is in the moment. Wow! is acknowledging that it is all so fascinating and unknown and fun. Wow! is an exhilarating way to live.

—Anna R.

***

This is a handy-dandy all-purpose tool! In my experience, "Wow!" is useful and appropriate in almost any situation that isn't calm and peaceful. It enables me to shift gears in an instant from whatever trigger might be presenting itself and to ground myself in the "is-ness" of the moment with awareness and appreciation for what I or someone else has created. For me, what follows is: "wow and allow," which shifts me into neutral observation.

—Janice

You to you – U2U (comparing)

Stop and pat yourself on the back every once in a while, won't you? Your inner truth is externalized through your life, and a lot of times it's the crappy bits that you notice. But we want you to start paying attention to the bits that reflect an internal journey that's actually moving toward bliss, that's actually on a transformational path. Because that's the truth of it. The truth of it is that you're on a transformational path and things are changing and it's easy to get lost in the changes if they're challenging. But the truth is, comparing you to you, you are transforming. And you need to be patting yourself on the back, giving yourself credit, and mentioning to your friends the things that are transforming in you in order to give them the kind of publicity within you that the shitty bits get. Publicize your transformation. Or at least notice it, at a minimum.

You are constantly in a pattern of transformation. If you don't do compare you to you, you're likely to feel like you are in one never-ending problem. When you compare you to you, you stop for a moment to realize, "Well, this is a different thing I'm dealing with now. That other issue shifted, so maybe I can try those tools with this new trigger."

***

Veronica writes:

This tool has such a loving feeling to it. You are making progress. You are transforming. You are changing. It is happening. Stop and allow yourself to see it. Love yourself for the progress you have made. Be fascinated by the journey yet to come.

***

I'm so focused on moving forward all the time, I sometimes forget to do this. But when I remember this tool, I love myself for who I am—again.

   —Randy Sue Collins

***

Compare you to you allows me to step out of an old situation and instantly reevaluate it with a fresh outlook.

   —Mike

***

Comparing me to me in stressful situations has been both fascinating and encouraging. There is always a gem of progress to be seen and felt that keeps my heart light and gives me courage to keep on keeping on.

   —Deb

***

I find this tool extremely helpful in measuring my progress over time. How would a similar issue have affected me in the past? "Compare you to you" is a perfect measuring stick for gauging personal growth.

   —Murster

***

Compare U2U is such an affirming tool. It is so great to feel the progress I'm making. It is so sweet and so fair to leave everyone else out of the picture and just relish how far I've come. Nothing inspires like success, right?

   —Anna R., Mexico

Terms

2012

The year 2012 is a shifting point on your calendar, a place of attention in order to help you focus. This is not a deadline, but a focal point to help facilitate your desire for consciousness and your desire for transformation. It is not a fixed point in time. The "place" of 2012 is a potential for dramatic transformation. That "place" is meeting you where you are; from there, you create the transformation that you desire both as a human and as a soul.

3D

Shorthand term for expressing the soul incarnate in the physical form, experiencing duality, density, and running the fear-based operating system. 3D is the status quo human condition prior to the shift to Homo spiritus.

4 billion

There are at least 4 billion people on the planet who won't agree with you, won't like you, or will never meet you. This number is likely underestimated. When we say, "Oh, you have found one of the 4 billion," it is not to dismiss or diminish their views, but to comfort you that this is a common phenomenon and put it into a perspective that hopefully helps you manage any triggers that come up. The energetics of this idea are similar to saying, "There are other fish in the sea."

5D

Shorthand term for expressing the soul experiencing the human form with a consciousness-based operating system. 5D is the experience of Homo spiritus, where the body is lived from an ensouled perspective.

Abundance

Abundance and "your abundant nature" are terms to describe the energetics reflecting the dynamic scope of possibility offered at this time, a concept meant to reflect the infinite possibilities (of all types) that exist in your physical world.

Our favorite way to illustrate the concept of true abundance is to have people look at how much nature surrounds them, for example: grass, trees, air, sky, and clouds. When one finds oneself lacking abundance, it is important to remember that abundance always exists in nature, and that is the place to start. You can also look at people smiling, hair on people's heads, or how many people have shoes. The point is to find a way to look into the world and see that there is much abundance.

The term abundance has also been corrupted to mean great sums of money or hoarding. Abundance, as an expanded definition, requires that one breaks the cycle or releases the belief that abundance only reflects how much money one has or how many houses one owns, to instead reflect any place where there is plenty or plentiful-ness. One simply needs to shift one's perspective about what plenty or abundance is.

Aha

A moment of clarity and insight that comes from accessing the soul's perspective; contrast this with the repetitive hamster-wheel-mind habit of thinking.
Ahas are commonly experienced while in the shower or doing other tasks that don't require full attention. The path of ascension and the choice for consciousness facilitate experiencing a steady stream of ahas.

Akashic Record
The galactic Internet.

A term that reflects the totality of: all of the lifetimes of those who have experienced Earth, all of the time that one has spent between lifetimes, all of the time spent in other incarnational opportunities, and all the time spent as a soul doing whatever the soul wanted to do. Think of a giant library where you each have your own section or file containing everything that has ever been recorded regarding what you've done, how you've lived, and what you've encountered. This isn't kept in anything that would resemble a library but it is helpful to think of it in this way conceptually.

Your Akashic Record is a reservoir of information that makes up the body of your soul. The energy that reflects that reservoir of information is what would be correlated to the physicality of the soul, if the soul had physicality.

When you are not in body and encounter another soul, your section of the Akashic Records is the information presented to the other soul. Your Akashic Record is the information that your soul presents to other souls at first glance.

Alternate expressions

Your "past and future" lives. Since time is not linear, these so-called "past and future" lives are all happening simultaneously; therefore your "other" lives can be referred to as alternate expressions of you.

Amnesia

The term we use to describe the "clean slate" of forgetfulness that a human experiences to facilitate living in physical form. It is a necessary state of being to incarnate into the physical body. Amnesia allows you to focus on the present moment in the present lifetime, without distractions from other lifetimes.

If you did not have amnesia about previous Earth experiences and incarnations it would be virtually impossible to stay in the moment because you'd be too busy wanting to go finish, redo, or undo things that have happened in alternate expressions.

Appreciation brings you into the moment

The high-vibrational space of love, appreciation, and fascination stops the thinking and clears the way for your soul's insight to drop in.

By appreciating yourself, you bring yourself into the space where you love yourself well. Appreciation is a very high-vibrational state. It's quite magnetic; it attracts other high-vibrational states.

Ascension

Ascension is a gradual, albeit drastic, transformation from a fear-based operating system into a consciousness-based operating system. Ascension requires evolution in the physical form and a radical shift in the way you respond to the biological messages the body offers.

Ascension is the term assigned to the energetic of the evolutionary leap into Homo spiritus. The Homo spiritus energetic allows for a life to be lived from the soul's perspective, and for a transformed way of interacting with physical matter.

Ascension does not mean you're leaving the body or the planet. Ascension means you're experiencing being in-body on Earth in a brand-new way that is a higher-vibrational, conscious way of living from your soul's perspective in which a spiritual partnership is formed between the soul, physical form, and personality self.

Audience or opinion

Sometimes, people just want an audience for their ramblings/complaining and aren't actually looking for connection. Be cautious about matching energy and lowering your vibration in these situations.

Aura

A way of describing the energy field that surrounds objects, people, animals, and even places. Another way of describing the emanation of individuality; the emanation of the truth of you.

A person's aura is most easily perceivable 4–8 feet from the body; however, auras extend out infinitely.

Baggage

The past, future, cultural pressures, DNA pressures, habits, triggers, and other static that get in the way of you experiencing the moment.

Being a question mark

Each of you has a question that you have incarnated to explore. The broad way of stating this question is, "Who am I?"

You're a question. Your soul asks a question and the exploration of the question—not the answer, but the exploration of the question—is you and your purpose of being in the body at this time.

"What is the question I am answering by the current way I am living?

What is the question I'm exploring by my expression?" consciously knowing you are in a questioning state is very important. Nothing is actually certain. When you make peace with certainty being a fallacy, you then say, "Well, what am I experiencing instead?"

You're in the question of you as you anticipate clarity coming in, not to answer the question but to give you the next step on the road of exploring the question that you are living. Clarity is not a stopping point. It is not a substitute for what you hoped certainty would be. It is simply an "aha" on the road of exploring the question of you that your soul is asking.

The question "Who am I?" does not go away simply because you have an aha about it in this moment. The question continues to exist. The questioning state is a permanent condition of your soul's nature.

"Who am I?" "Aha" and, "Who am I?" That's the path of consciousness. "Why am I here? Why am I doing this? Why, why, why, why?" The why doesn't need an answer. It is not about an outcome. Exploration of the why is a way to access the ever-unfolding truth of you. Your state of being is: "I am in why."

Bliss

The state of living in a spiritual partnership with your soul as a high-vibrational, conscious being. The state resulting from having tools for conscious living, being in neutral observation, and knowing that an experience previously judged as wrong (or right) is actually an opportunity for learning and growth. Living in a state of bliss is the result of living in the consciousness-based operating system as Homo spiritus.

Boundaries

Using your ability as a creator while living in a free-will zone to choose what you are interested in experiencing; directing the incarnation.

Boundaries with consequences

In order to leave fear, victimhood, and low-vibrational states behind, you set boundaries in the moment—boundaries with consequences. Boundaries without consequences are just hot air coming out of your mouth. For example, you might say, "You can't speak to me that way," and then the person speaks to you that way. If you don't then act (enact the consequences), all you're doing is blowing hot air. So, boundaries should have consequences attached for the person you're setting the boundary with: "This is what's acceptable in my life and if that doesn't work for you, then you're not in my life."

Is it hard to say to someone, "I'm setting a boundary with you and there are consequences attached"? Of course it is. Is it hard to continue the relationship without boundaries and feel like a victim all the time? We think that's harder.

Brain

Your brain is the biological functioning unit for thinking and it runs the body's processes. The brain also allows you to experience insight.

Bunnies and rainbows

You don't always have to put a smiley face on everything in order to be liked, loved, appreciated, understood, companioned. The way we like to say this is: It doesn't all have to be bunnies and rainbows.

EXAMPLES OF HOW THIS TERM IS USED:

You have to know what the truth of heart chakra energy is, and it's not bunnies and rainbows. It's not just love, love, love. It's loving yourself first.

***

The high-vibrational aspect of this situation isn't necessarily bunnies and rainbows. It's not, "I only want the bunnies and rainbows kind of thing out of that alternate expression." It's, "I want what's going to make me higher-vibrational, more conscious, in the now." So if you find yourself unable to love aspects of yourself, well, welcome to the shadowland. Welcome to an aspect of knowing what you need to work with. Why don't you love it? How can you say, "I love you" to that aspect of you? We are not going to fall for any, "I love you because you are bright and shiny and bunnies and rainbows." If you don't love something about yourself it is more conscious to say, "I don't love me" than it is to say, "Well I'm going to love me" or "I have to say I love me."

***

It's not as much that you have to say "I need to love it" or "I need it to have light" or any of those things. It's not, "OK, yes, my knee hurts; let's get the bunnies and rainbows out." It's, "Yes, my knee hurts and it's teaching me." So, say yes to what it is and then work with it, but continue to remind yourself of that "yes" to what it is.

***

The moment isn't a bunnies-and-rainbows spot, and a lot of times in some of the literature that's out there they say, "Oh, just be in the moment and all will be well." Well, that's crap. Be in the moment and you will start to experience the intensity that's available to you as a Homo spiritus individual. It is intense and it does ask a lot of you, but that's why you have lots and lots of tools to support your journey. The moment isn't necessarily going to be silence. It's not meditation. It's an opening to an enormous amount of insight, an enormous amount of information, and an enormous amount of opportunity to live differently in the *next* moment, to create differently for the *next* moment, to move differently into the *next* moment.

***

"Perfect" doesn't mean "feels good." Perfect is not bunnies and rainbows. Perfect is not easy. What is perfect? Precisely what is needed to give you the handhold on the climbing wall of ascension that you need right now.

***

Healing is an interesting word. By healing we don't necessarily mean: "Is it happy, happy, joy, joy, bunnies and rainbows?" No. By healing we mean: "Do I grow? Do I transform? Do I like myself more? Do I feel like I'm a better person? Am I becoming more of the truth of me?"

But and because

We use "but and because" as a red flag to alert you that you may be slipping into victim mentality. If you find yourself using those words, you may be leaving the realm of "I created it" and entering into the position of "it was done to me." Listen to conversation around you and begin to notice how frequently you hear "because this" and "but that."

At times, you may feel like you need to include a "but" or a "because" to feel like you have conveyed your entire story. That may be the case. We are not saying that you should remove them from your language completely. We are suggesting that you become conscious of how you use "but" and "because." We believe it will help uncover places where you are habituating to victimhood.

You said, "Yeah, I have 35 different ways money comes to me, *but* I still can't pay my bills." Instead say, "I have 35 ways money comes to me. Period."

"But and because" take away your high-vibrational state, they lower your energetic, make it more difficult to reach insight from your soul, and cause you to slip back into thinking, thinking, thinking. Remember, if thinking could have solved it, it would've solved it long ago, because you sure have thought about it enough. We aren't looking to think more, we are seeking insight.

You are tempted to say: "Oh, but I couldn't; oh, but I don't; oh, but that's silly; oh, but, oh, but." Right? It does not serve you to "but-and-because" away a fascination. A fascination is present for a reason. The exploration of the fascination is the gift, the gift you give yourself. What exactly do you think your soul's perspective is going to feel like? Souls are very curious. They want to learn and grow and do new things. Is it surprising that the soul's perspective comes in as fascination and curiosity?

Certainty

When you are operating from the fear-based operating system, change feels extremely risky. The survival instinct is constantly pressuring you to stay the same, because "the same" has kept you alive. Any changes to "the same" require certainty about the outcome in order to quiet the fears the survival instinct produces. As certainty is a fallacy—you can't be truly certain of anything in the diverse, vast world you find yourself in—you find yourself in a no-win situation: Change requires certainty, certainty is unattainable, and paralysis (fear) is the result.

Evolving your relationship to the survival instinct and certainty is a major aspect of the ascension process.

Chakra

Energy centers in the body. Traditionally, there are seven major chakras: Root (1st), Sexuality (2nd), Power (3rd), Heart (4th), Throat (5th), Third eye (6th), and Crown (7th). We use the idea of chakras as a handy reference tool. It's a shortcut that allows us to talk about different aspects of your body and energetic system without having to go into a long explanation each time. It is not required that you believe in chakras to follow the conversation.

Change

The recognition of an altered condition in the incarnation, which, if processed habitually, often triggers fear. When processed consciously, change becomes the mechanism for growth.

Channel

An incarnated soul experiencing the human form that allows non-physical guides to communicate through him or her in order to present helpful information in a palatable form. If out-of-body or non-corporal guides showed up as a burning bush, beam of light, or in a light body of some fashion, they would be far more likely to create fear than comfort. Channeling and channels allow a more human-to-human type of transmission of information, commonly less triggering than other types of transmissions.

Channeled message

Information that comes through a channel from guides that are not in physical form, but have perspective on the physical journey or the human experiment.

Checking things off your list

You incarnated into this lifetime with what we call a "list" of things that you hoped to do. The list includes experiences you wanted to have, things that you were interested in doing, unfinished business, experiences that you wanted to try again, or plans you made with other souls. You and your soul started this list before you ever incarnated into the physical form and it has carried over throughout all the incarnations you have experienced here on Earth.

What tends to happen is that as things on your list "come up," you check off the things that are less triggering, less challenging, and less difficult first. The items that are more difficult are often passed over to be dealt with another time. As you get closer and closer to the last few items on your list, they can feel very difficult. They feel more difficult because every time you said, "Oh no! I'm not ready to do that item right now, I'm going to do something else!" the item acquired a charge of impossibility. If you have re-queued the same issue many times, the charge of impossibility can feel quite large.

A lot of you have several things that have been on your list over many lifetimes of which you are very energetically frightened. Every time they've come up, you haven't been able to handle them. Now that you're at a higher-vibrational level than you've ever been with more awareness and tools, these things don't need to be anywhere near as scary as they used to be. In fact, you are more prepared to handle them than you have ever been before. In essence, you were clever by procrastinating! How often do you get to hear that?

The tricky part is that although you are now energetically prepared to experience these last few things on your list, the habit of fright is so deep that it can get in the way of looking at it from today's perspective and being able to say, "What's really going on here?" It's easy to lose sight of the fact that you have more tools and ability to handle them than ever before, but once you wade into them, they usually are much easier to deal with than you had imagined. It's just about being courageous enough to experience them after so many lifetimes of being so fearful.

Choose your reactions to your creations

"I am 100 percent responsible for my reactions to my creations." That's one of the most conscious things you can say. We strongly recommend that you write that down and stick it on your bathroom mirror.

"I am a creator; I created it all. It's all here *for* me, and I choose how I react to my creations as well." When something occurs, don't look for it to be different. Don't say, "I wish it were some other way." Say, "What is here right now is here on purpose. It's here because it needs to be here to facilitate my growth." Then, take it further; take your acknowledgment of the truth of you as a creator to the point where you can also say, "I am choosing the reaction I have to every single experience in my life. All of it."

It is your responsibility to set boundaries, state preferences, tell the truth about your creations, and to make sure that your creations bring out the authenticity of you, which you can then share. That's the gift of creating and choosing your reactions to your creations; it lets you share the truth of you. Consistently emanate the truth of you regardless of the circumstances you find yourself in by choosing your reactions based on your high-vibrational, conscious experiences of yourself.

Compassion

The traditional use of this word is very low-vibrational, as it tends toward victimization. Every experience is here to teach you something. Every experience is here as an opportunity for growth. When you feel compassion for someone, be very cautious that you are not casting them as a victim of their circumstances. You can say, "Wow, that seems like a tough way to learn, can I support you as you experience it?" But it is low-vibrational to say, "I feel sorry for you," or any other comment that implies the situation wasn't chosen.

This isn't a very romantic way to express what has been termed compassion, and may even feel harsh. However, you are either a victim or a creator. You can't be both. Exploring your creations (even if you have no conception of why you would have created them) is the path of consciousness and ascension.

Complex vs. complicated

Complex is fine. Complex is interesting. Complex is plenty of stuff going on and your brain likes it and your body likes it and your soul, of course, likes it.

Complicated is static. Complicated is low vibration. Complicated is unconscious. Complicated is, "Oh God, I have to make sure this person is happy," and "Oh God, I have to look after that person," and "Oh God..." this, that and the other thing. Complicated doesn't serve you.

Complex fascinates you. Complicated confuses you.

Complicated feels like there are no answers. Complex feels like "Oh, I get to put this puzzle together." Complicated feels like "All the puzzle pieces are the same color and someone's screaming at me while I'm trying to build it."

So, use "complicated" as a red flag. When it's complicated, look closely; it's an opportunity to become more conscious!

Conscious/Consciousness

Knowing why you do what you do. Choosing your reactions. Not being driven by habit. Experiencing the world as a creator rather than as a victim.

The world, as you experience it, has been programmed through habits, fears, and your biology. Through attention (consciousness), you can live the bigger picture that includes your personality's paradigm shifting and the embracing of your soul's perspective, as well.

Consciousness-based operating system (CBOS)

The consciousness-based operating system is the 5-D or Homo spiritus way of experiencing the world that allows for conscious interactions with experiences rather than fear-based, habitually driven interaction with experiences.

Core Emotion (CE)

Your core emotion is a theme present in every thought, action, feeling, dream, hope, experience, and desire. It is present in all moments of your life. Your core emotion is unique to you and unique to this lifetime. Discovering your core emotion often answers long-standing questions such as: "Why does this keep happening?" "Why do all my relationships follow the same pattern?" "Why can't I get past this blockage in my path?"

Most people experience their core emotion from an unconscious or un-healed perspective. Learning to work with your core emotion from a healed or conscious perspective is often described as "life-changing." Since the core emotion is present in all aspects of your life, bringing conscious-ness to the core emotion brings consciousness to all aspects of your life.

NOTE: The exploration of your core emotion is one of our specialties. We have a specific process for revealing your core emotion and helping you move from an unhealed to a healed relationship with it. Because of the intensely personal nature of this exploration and the time required to fully explore it, we only offer this process through private sessions. For more information, see the contact page.

Courage

Awareness of the temptation to fear and other types of static, but making the choice to act from consciousness instead.

Courageous enough

Are you courageous enough to think about now instead of running habit with the hamster-wheel mind? Are you courageous enough to think about this moment rather than skipping over it?

Creating your reality

"Create your own reality" is one of those terms that's overused and under-understood. Creating your reality is often believed to be a way to *control* your reality. It is thought to be a path to certainty and safety. Creating your reality is actually an outcome of your vibrational self, your vibrational nature, your emanation of a higher-vibrational choice.

Creating your reality works very much like a fountain. The fountain shoots up the water and it sprays out all over the place. No one knows where every drop's going to land. Who would want to? It would be tedious in the extreme. The uncertainty creates the beauty.

Similarly, creating your reality isn't about the outcome (where the drops land), it is about the experience (the beauty of the water in the air.)

In our fountain example, the water represents the truth of you (your soul's perspective and your personality), the water pressure represents your free-will choices and the fountain mechanism represents your preferences and boundaries.

Creating your reality starts with setting boundaries in association with your preferences. You then align your free-will to choose conscious reactions to your experiences (which often has the result of clearing static), and then you and your soul emanate together.

You initiate your creation, you choose how you react to your creation, and you remain open to insight from your soul.

Creator, The

If you believe that this world is created, then there must be a Creator. Therefore, the Creator is the one who created all. It helps to recognize that the Creator is not conceivable in its entirety while experiencing duality because of the inherent limitations of the human mind and the infinite scope of the Creator. However, the Creator can be sensed through insight from your soul and through experiencing creation.

Creator/creatorship

As a creator, you are aware that you are in a free-will zone and that you have the ability to choose your reactions to your experiences. When creations seem to be in opposition to what you "want," creators recognize that there are levels of creation and that everything is happening *for* me, rather than falling into victimhood.

Cultural pressures

Cultural pressures include: family beliefs, societal norms, and customs. Often, cultural pressures present as, "It's what everyone else is doing" and are used to justify forgoing transformation.

Habits and DNA pressures combine with cultural pressures to make a potent combination for habitual response to triggers.

Density

Experiencing the free-will zone in a body. Souls do not have physical form in the same way humans do. Incarnating on Earth provides for the unique experience of density, duality, and free will.

Digging a ditch

If you've been digging a ditch for 50 years, it's pretty easy to dig it deeper. You already have the walls there, you already have the guidelines and the exact dimensions of the ditch, and you have a plan.

If you decide that you're going to dig a ditch in a new area, it requires a different kind of attention. You start off by marking the lines where you want the ditch to be. Then you need to figure out where you're going to take the dirt you remove, etc. The new project requires many new actions and perhaps even some new tools.

It's the same with changing habitual responses.

Instead of repeating old patterns, you're starting a whole new journey. That changeover requires some consistency. Sure, you can always go back to the "comfortable" old ditch, but we're pretty sure you have learned all you need to learn about that. Use spiritual discipline to focus on new, healthy patterns to get out of the old rut and open up your life.

DNA pressures

Your DNA is the blueprint for your body. You and your soul collaborated to create the unique incarnation you are experiencing.

We use the term "DNA pressures" to refer to the interaction habits and consciousness have with your physicality.

As an example: Tall people habitually put things on high shelves while shorter people will habitually put things on lower shelves. Both are examples of people acting based on DNA (and convenience).

DNA pressures combine with cultural pressures to make a potent combination for habitual response to triggers.

Don't bring your baggage to the moment

Your ability to neutrally observe your life without bringing anything to the moment. You don't gather things up from your past. You don't pull things in from the future. You don't allow your fears to be involved. You say, "What is this moment? I am experiencing only *this* moment."

Duality

The idea that there are only two options, typically experienced as either, "what I think is right and what I think is wrong," or "what they think is right and what they think is wrong." A very limited way to experience Earth and the human form. The fear-based operating system loves duality because it gives a false sense of certainty. (I am RIGHT). The consciousness-based operating system leaves duality behind as it explores the truth of, "Everything that happens, happens for me and is teaching me something."

Earth

The planet Earth is designated as a free-will zone and was developed to provide opportunities for incarnating souls to experience density and duality. Earth, at this time, is engaged in an ascension process and will reflect a changed environment for ascended beings to explore. What that changed environment will actually look like is unknown, and highly anticipated for that very reason.

Ease

Living in the human form while utilizing tools for conscious living.

Ease not easy

We never said it would be easy to ensoul your physical form and evolve your body. We never promised "easy," but we did commit to you that you could start living in ease.

Easy

Please, please, please, give up on the idea that "easy" means you're right or that "easy" means it's working. It's not about easy, meaning: no effort. It's about realization, moving through, handling and processing triggers, recognizing transformation, and allowing change in.

Allowing change in is almost always the final step because things start to shake out inside of you, you start to create in your external world, and then all of a sudden something has to change. Your relationship to your world starts to shift. And if you're not willing to take that final step and shift your relationship to your world, then you've done all that work and you're not actually enjoying it or experiencing it.

Part of what happens is you think, "Well, if it's not easy, it's not worth doing," or "It's not easy, so I don't want to," or "It's not easy, so I'm on the wrong path." It's not about easy. It's about looking at your world and saying, "I'm triggered and I want to transform it," or "this habit that I'm not happy with, I want to make it different," and then paying attention to it, which allows you to shift it and transform it into something else. That's the freedom here—paying attention to the thing that you become aware of and then sticking with it enough that you allow your life to shift around the change you've made.

What we really see happen is that you do a ton of internal work and then when it starts to appear in your world, asking you for something new, you resist the external change. There is the temptation to stay small even though the work has been done. The temptation to stay small has to be dealt with. That means taking the internal work and experiencing it externally, walking it, emanating it. Don't drop the ball on the last step. Because that's really where the rubber meets the road. Until then, it's all personal, but when you take it into the world, there can be that last little hurdle. At some point you have to stick your neck out in order to experience your changed life.

Eloheim

We, the Eloheim, are a collaboration of souls presenting with a singular voice, channeled through the body of Veronica Torres with her explicit approval, willingness, and allowance. It is our great privilege to offer our support to you at this very exciting time on Earth to facilitate the transformation of Homo sapiens to Homo spiritus; moving from the fear-based operating system to the consciousness-based operating system. It is a grand experiment that many beings in the universe are watching with great interest, awe, and fascination.

Emanating (the truth of you)

As you live consciously, you emanate consciousness into your world. Your job is just to contribute, your job is not to try to dictate or control where your contribution to high-vibrational living ends up. It's not your business where it goes or how it shows up in the world.

Energetics

The way that souls communicate through nonverbal knowing. Because your physical forms cannot yet communicate on the level that souls do, nonverbal knowing or "energetics" need to be translated into your language to facilitate understanding and communication.

Since it is always less accurate to use language than it is to communicate energetically, it is our hope and desire that your progress will eventually include the ability to communicate energetically without the need for language.

Energetic communication is happening all the time. Living consciously means that you are emanating a conscious energetic. It really does matter how you handle triggers and other upsets. Not just because it determines how you will experience the triggers, but it also determines how your emanation will go out to others. When we work with you, we are reading your energetics far more than we are listening to your words. Your energetics often show us visuals, which we can use to facilitate deeper understanding of the situations you are experiencing.

Ensoulment

The process by which soul energy is more deeply experienced by the personality incarnated in the physical form as the perspective is shifted from one of a survival instinct to a soul's perspective—from a fear-based operating system to a consciousness-based operating system.

Ensoulment, or living from the soul's perspective, is a collaboration between the personality self (you incarnate as a human) and your soul's wisdom. Don't misunderstand this to be that your soul "takes you over." This is not the case.

As an example, let's say you take a calculus class. The you at the end of the class hasn't 'taken over' the you from the beginning of the class. You have become a being that has the additional experience of the wisdom you gained in your studies.

Ensoulment is you realizing the wisdom and insight your soul already has; the completeness of you.

Fear

Fear is a biological reaction to change or the idea of change that typically creates the "fight or flight" response in the body, which is an adrenaline-based response to, "What do I do next?" Typically, the answer is that you run habit.

Consciously experiencing fear presents opportunities for extreme growth because it gives you the opportunity to break habitual patterns—to experience the moment rather than experiencing habit, which often involves projection of the future or bringing a memory of the past into the moment.

Fear can also be defined as the biological component of duality. It is the biological response to the belief in duality that is enacted regardless of which side of duality you're on. If you're on the side of duality that says, "This is wrong," then there's fear for survival. If you're on the side that says, "This is right," there's fear that it won't continue.

Fear and the survival instinct work together to keep you small.

Fear-based

Actions based on fear rather than conscious choice, a habitual, unconscious mentality (operating system) based on fear.

Fear-based operating system (FBOS)

You are a fear-based being. It is not something you can argue. It is a fact. Period. Full stop. End of sentence. You cannot argue with the fact that you are a fear-based being because you have been built to operate from fear in order to continue surviving. You've been built to startle at loud noises. You've been built to have the fight-or-flight response trigger in you. You've been built to be wary and aware of your surroundings. All of this can be summarized or reduced to fear. There is no need to be ashamed of admitting the fears that you find yourself experiencing because it is a core aspect of being human. You were brought into this incarnation running the fear-based operating system, meaning you're constantly experiencing the world based on fear. The survival instinct is continuously asking you to be wary. The survival instinct is continuously trying to keep you small and it has extreme measures it can go to in order to keep you from sticking your neck out, from standing out in the crowd, from being noticed. The survival instinct flares up in you and requires your habitual responses to stimulus and triggers.

As consciousness is applied to the fear-based operating system, and as you break out of habitual response patterns, you're able to experience what is going on in your life from a new perspective and shift into a consciousness-based operating system.

Fear is a choice not a mandate

A high-vibrational reaction to a fear. Watch fear occur in your life. Watch it, watch it, choose and choose again to see it a different way, to see it rather than feel it.

Your reaction to an experience is a choice and not an inevitability. Fear is a choice, and so is fascination.

Fire hose

We use this term to refer to situations where strong emotions are acted out in unconscious ways. When you "fire hose," it's as though you are "spraying" your emotions onto those around you.

We frequently see this pattern with people who are learning to set boundaries. They find themselves in a situation they want to change, but are hesitant to act. They wait to act, which causes the feelings to build to a breaking point. When they finally do set a boundary, it is often accompanied by shouting, anger, throwing things, or other intense behaviors. A boundary was set, but it was done from a low-vibrational place.

Healthy, high-vibrational, boundary setting is an extremely important part of the spiritual journey. To do this, live consciously, know the truth of you in this moment, and act upon it quickly.

Free will

Free will is the opportunity to be in amnesia about the truth of you: the truth of your infinite, immortal nature.

Free will allows you to experience Earth as YOU see fit. No one can interfere with your chosen experience—not your soul, and not even The Creator.

Note, we said your chosen experience. You choose how you experience everything. Your free will gives you this ability. Now, we are not saying that everything that happens in your life feels like something you have chosen on a personality level; however, your chosen reaction to everything that happens in your life is within your purview.

Free will gives you the option to break out of the fear-based operating system, to break habits, exercise change and choose consciousness.

Free-will zone

An experiment that was initiated by The Eloheim after being invited by The Creator to come up with something new for souls to experience. It is an opportunity for souls to incarnate in a completely amnesic state and live a lifetime through their own direction, without influence from external forces, to grow as a soul. The free-will zone is inclusive of the solar system that holds Earth.

Fulfillment

Grace, ease, and bliss; living in the physical form and running the consciousness-based operating system, while having a spiritual partnership with the soul.

Gate latch

The sound that happens when a gate swings shut and the latch hooks. When we speak with you and you come to understand a concept, we hear a gate latch sound. Sometimes, we feel the change in you and then we hear the sound.

God

A word used to describe the concept of an all-knowing Creator, but can be interpreted to mean anything. God is a word defined by the individual according to his or her experience. There is not one definition for everyone. To say the word "God" and expect others to understand what you intend to mean by that word is too open to misinterpretation. To avoid this, we recommend using at least 10 words to convey complex spiritual concepts such as "God."

Going to see the king

We use this phrase to describe your interactions with authority figures.

AN EXAMPLE:

You want to speak to your boss about a promotion. How do you approach "going to see the king"? It is essential that when you "go to see the king," or anyone else for that matter, that you bring your high-vibrational, conscious self to the encounter. Keep "What is true now?" as your focus. Remember, when you encounter an authority figure, don't let their response to you tell you who you are. Emanate the truth of you, focus on this moment, state preferences, set boundaries, and remember that it is all happening *for* you.

When you go to see the king, whomever the king is in your world, if you show up authentically you've done your part to contribute to a conscious conversation. If you encounter people who know who they are and present themselves authentically—whether it's a king or a boss or a baker—you can trust the exchange to be high-vibrational or at least conscious or at a minimum not generating more static. If they don't do their half, well, that's something very, very important to know about them, isn't it?

Going with the flow

Comment: "I'm going to go with the flow; I'll just deal with things as they come up."

Response: Be cautious about this idea. "The flow" is often a "path of least resistance," a low-vibrational energetic.

Comment: What I meant is, "I'm going to be conscious about whatever comes up."

Response: Great, say that instead. It makes a big difference. There is an energetic pattern in the idea of "going with the flow" that is a mismatch with who you are now. Saying, "I'll attend to what arises," OK, that's fine. Saying, "I'll be conscious about what shows up," OK, that's good. Saying, "I'll go with the flow." Nope. Why?

Too frequently, "going with the flow" results in you forgetting to set boundaries because the idea is, "Well, whatever happens I'll just flow with it!" This is not a recommended activity.

We are not suggesting you become rigid; we love for you to explore uncertainty! What we are recommending is that you continue to be conscious as you explore flexibility. Even if you are experiencing someone else's plans, you can still stand with the intention of observing and making choices, setting boundaries, stating preferences, and using your free will to explore your reactions to your creations.

Grace

Grace is living your life knowing that everything that is happening is happening for your growth. "I gracefully recognize this experience is here to teach me. I don't have to approach this as a victim. I can approach this as a creator." That's being in a state of grace.

Growth

Consciousness infusing the incarnation, resulting in transformation.

Guides

A generic or general term used for beings that are not currently in physical form that are available to assist those who are in physical form, through a variety of means—through channels, through coincidence, through synchronicities, through dreams, and many other ways.

Habit/Habitual response

Habit is tied into the fear of getting dead and the survival instinct. Since the body is programmed to stay alive, it will say, "Well, this hasn't killed me yet, so let's continue." Change makes the body feel like there's a potential to get killed. Change means new factors to manage, new things to deal with, and new situations to juggle. It is easier on the body if it already knows the threats that are involved in your day-to-day life and has already established that none of them are threatening enough to get you dead. The body is going to want to keep repeating that pattern. If you know that a food is poisonous to you, you don't eat it again—making that a healthy habit. But the survival instinct, as translated into 21st-century Earth, ends up looking like, "I can't quit this job that I hate because I'm too afraid of getting dead. I'm too engrained in this habit to try something else."

Hamster-wheel thinking

The habitual mind repetitiously trying to think its way out of "problems." Repetitious thinking about past and/or future experiences misses the experience of the moment.

Healing

Consciousness-infused biological responses and choices which create growth and a transformed experience of the body.

Heart–power chakra combination

From a soul's perspective, your heart chakra (4th) and power chakra (3rd) are combining. We see the energy flow as a figure-8 pattern, or an infinity symbol.

There's no longer a difference between acting from your heart chakra and acting from your power chakra. This means that you no longer go out into the world expecting to gain if others are going to lose from your actions. You no longer go out in the world knowing that you could be powerful at the expense of others. The idea of climbing over someone else to get to what you want becomes as distasteful as murder, or rape, or arson, or anything that you personally have a big problem with. You are not able to function in the world in a way that is not within your own integrity. You can't cheat a little on the side. You can't sneak down and operate from your power chakra, ignoring your heart chakra for a few hours and then expect to jump back to the heart chakra and ignore the power chakra. You can't play that game anymore. Consciousness illuminates the truth of them working in teamwork and it says there's no way you can be in the world without being from your integrity, being from your authenticity, and being from your wholeness.

Heart chakra energy has often times been out of balance—either "I serve, I love, I give," especially women, "I give, give, give,"—or your heart's closed down. There's been a lot of out-of-balance heart chakra energy on this planet.

When the power chakra gets out of balance it tends to be either "I'm going to go take care of business," with a corporate-raider kind of energy, or you have no boundaries and you're a victim.

The merging of the heart and power chakras addresses this imbalance. When you bring in the density of the power chakra and combine it with the etheric nature of the heart chakra, together they operate from a more balanced state. That's really the beauty of it.

The combined chakra can be called the ensouled chakra or the ensoulment chakra. It's the chakra where the energetic center of the body emanates out into the world.

High-vibrational

High-vibrational refers to actions, thoughts, ideas, and relationships which are based on consciousness and conscious choices. It is not a judgmental term; rather it is descriptive of the fact that your body is actually vibrating at a different rate than it did before you infused consciousness into your life.

Your soul vibrates at a very high rate. Raising your vibration by living consciously is a very important step in living from your soul's perspective and walking the path of ascension.

Hoarding

One of the most low-vibrational states you experience. "I'm going to look out for me and I don't care what happens to other people." Hoarders are constantly in lack and looking for how they can get more. They are obsessed by the question, "How can I get what I don't have?" They never feel like they have enough of what they need.

Homo spiritus

A name for a state of being that is possible when you live in collaboration with your soul incorporating your soul's perspective; a transformed, expanded experience of the physical form and a shifted paradigm of how one is on Earth.

Living from the consciousness-based operating system, pursuing the path of ascension.

Insight

Information received directly from your soul.

The challenge when explaining the word "insight" is that it is a process that uses the brain but must not be confused with "thinking."

There are a few characteristics that illuminate the differences between the two: the mind is limited and will often present limiting messages. The mind's messages are repetitive and often negative. Insight will present ideas and options you've never considered before, which are always positive and constructive in their nature. Insight will never demean you; it will never be negative and it will always be supportive of your growth and transformation.

Jackets on the coat rack

Imagine that you have a row of jackets hanging on pegs by the front door. Each of these jackets represents an emotion. Just as you can choose which jacket you want to wear when you head out into the weather, you can choose which emotion you wish to experience.

Of course, this requires practice and spiritual discipline, but it is true: Every emotion is a choice.

What jacket will you wear today?

Joy

Joy is when you experience happiness without feeling like the other shoe is going to drop. You're just happy. And as you think, "Oh, but…" you don't let the "Oh, but…" have any airtime. Uncertainty makes joy possible. When you're comfortable with uncertainty, it is possible to be in joy. When you're comfortable with uncertainty, joy is possible because you don't require the situation to be a certain way in order for you to experience happiness, and prolonged happiness is joy.

Karma

The word "karma" had a strong definition coming out of Eastern religious beliefs. When it came to the West, the term became somewhat bastardized to mean, "If you're not good, something bad is going to happen to you."

Karma had a big duality perspective in it but if you take the duality out of it, it becomes, "Everything teaches me," instead of, "I'm waiting to get punished for any mistakes or slip-ups I make."

Lack

The idea that there is not enough. Lack is a fallacy; you live in an abundant universe. Lack is a sense of, "I should have more. Something is wrong or broken here." This is experiencing your life from a victim mentality. You are a creator; everything in your life is in your life to help you grow as a soul. As a creator, if you feel a sense of "not enough," look at it as an opportunity to uncover the actual blocks to your desire. We refer to these blocks as static and baggage. Living consciously is the path to clearing these blocks and experiencing your world in its true state, the state of abundance.

Landing

Spiritual growth tends to follow this pattern: periods of intense growth followed by periods that feel more like rests. We call these "resting" times being on the landing and the "growth" times climbing the stairs.

Lateral pass

It can be tempting to want to find a way to give responsibility for your experiences to someone else. This transfer of responsibility can look like: "I turn this problem over to my angels," or "I let my higher self deal with it," or even "God, take this burden from me!"

We call this making a lateral pass.

The assumption being made in this idea is that whomever you are making the lateral pass to is actually ready, willing, and able to do anything with your creation. You are in a free-will zone; we dispute that anyone or anything is here to take away your "problems" or that anyone or anything is better suited to interact with your creation than you are.

You created it so that you could learn from it. Why would you want to give it away? Does it feel too "hard" to deal with on your own? OK, that's why we have lots of tools to help you interact with your creations in new ways and from new perspectives. You are not alone in your exploration, but you are solely responsible for how you choose to react to your creations.

Layers of the onion

A quick way of saying that while issues may come up again and again, you are experiencing them at a deeper level each time.

Light worker

A soul incarnating at this time with the specific desire to grow spiritually and live consciously. A person walking the path of ascension. A Homo sapiens desiring to live as Homo spiritus.

Learning

As an incarnate soul, the processes that you go through in order to have the growth you desire are called "learning." The journey is a journey of change, shifts, transformation, and ascension, which is all brought into the physical system through the process of internal and external transformation, a reflection of all of the learning that has occurred.

Low-vibrational

A state of being that comes from living in the fear-based operating system, not looking for conscious understanding or an experience of the dynamics being presented to you. Living habitually rather than opening to new experience.

It is not a judgmental term; rather, it is descriptive of the fact that your body is actually vibrating at a different rate than it would if you infused consciousness into your life.

Your soul vibrates at a very high rate. It is difficult to connect to your soul's energy when living a low-vibrational life.

Marble sculpture

In a sense, bliss is inside of you. It's like Michelangelo carving a sculpture. The marble block is there; the sculpture is inside the block, not yet revealed. When you are in habit, you are looking at the block and thinking, "This could be more, this could be more, but that would require getting the tools out, it would require doing a lot of work, it would require, it would require..." and you find reasons not to change. Habit keeps you from seeing the beauty of the finished sculpture. All you get is the plain block. Now, if you want to get more out of your life, if you want to be that finished sculpture, the excess marble has to come off.

Just as the act of chipping away marble reveals the sculpture underneath, the act of attending to triggers and static reveals the highest version of you. When Michelangelo chipped a piece off the marble block, he didn't have to chip that same piece again; however, you often you have to go deeper and deeper and deeper in the same part of the block. That we know. But it is not that you do some work and then you have to do that work again. It's that you do some work and then sometimes you'll revisit that area to do deeper, finer work.

Sometimes, you've been working on the front and you haven't looked at the back in two years. And you turn the block around and you say, "Oh Lord, I'm really not attending to these things back here, am I? Well, I'm going to. I'm going to attend to them now. There were opportunities to look at this stuff before and I didn't, but I'm going to look at them now; in this moment, the current version of me is going to look at them now. I'm going to use my tools and take this opportunity to offer a different emanation and to transform static and triggers as I go."

You're clearing away the old rectangular-shaped block to reveal the beautiful figure that's always been there, just waiting for the accurate and consistent application of the appropriate tools to illuminate the beauty that only needed you to be willing to do the steps that unearth it, unveil it. You are there. You are the sculptor. And the consistency that you are willing to apply to the project tells the story. It allows the unfoldment.

The sculptor doesn't *build* the marble statue, it's something that's *revealed*—and that's what you're doing. You're revealing the integrity of you, meaning your soul expressed through the physical form, and the only way to reveal it is to remove that which isn't of the integrity of you.

It's the process of chipping and filing and buffing away the unwanted sections that reveals the sculpture. Being angry that the sculpture doesn't appear full-formed is ridiculous. When you find yourself in trigger or static—frustration, anger, anxiety, memories that trouble you—remember this idea that the sculpture doesn't show up fully formed. It's the journey of the discovery of the sculpture that is the meaningful part. When the sculpture is placed someplace in public and it emanates its beauty, then others get to experience it.

It does not get created until someone stands there and says, "I'm willing. I'm willing to chip off this section; I'm willing to buff this part out. I'm willing to scratch my head and wonder, 'Do I want an arm here or not?' I am willing." Your willingness to look at your static and triggers creates the beauty of you, which can then be emanated for an eternity. You have the marble block; you can be angry at it for not being finished or you can put your stamp on it. You can make it the vision you have. And then that vision will be emanated into the universe forever.

Stand in front of your unfinished self and decide what bits you want to keep and what bits you want to get rid of. Just as Michelangelo had the variety of tools that he used, you have tools to help you chip away the things you don't wish to see anymore. At some point you can stand there and say, "Comparing me to me, I have an arm now. Last year that was just a block but now you can actually see the fingers. You can see that I've decided how I want to be."

Math problem

If we ask: "What's 9,897,209.5 times 8,239,203?" you wouldn't take the first number that comes to mind as the right answer, but you'll take the first emotion that comes in as an indisputably correct position. If you find yourself in an emotion that doesn't seem actually relevant to the moment, be kind to yourself about it. Just remind yourself, "Oh yeah, that's right, the first emotion that trips along isn't necessarily the one I want to run with."

You can let yourself have the emotion, but know why you're having it. If all of a sudden, you feel sad or upset and you don't know why you're feeling that way, ask yourself, "Is there any good reason to be having this emotion? And if there isn't, then what can I ascertain about the state I'm in?" Remind yourself, "This emotion has no basis in reality, in the reality of this moment. This emotion is a choice."

Mind

The mind's thoughts and insight are both processed by the brain. The mind is only capable of taking the spiritual journey so far. At some point, the mind's ability to manage the spiritual journey comes to a standstill. Without the infusion of insight from the soul, the journey will stagnate. When you act, react, and create only from your mind, you're cutting yourself off from the vast resources of your soul and the Akashic Records. In this context, it's easy to see that allowing the mind to run the incarnation is limiting.

Mob mentality

Matching energy with low-vibrational states or low-vibrational people. Going with the flow. Acting habitually, as part of a group.

Money flows, not grows

Money flows, it doesn't grow. In the past, a lot of people have made their fortunes just by letting their money grow, but that was an old paradigm. Have you looked at interest rates lately? It doesn't work that way anymore, does it? Part of the reason for this change is the energetic truth of money is being revealed: high-vibrational money *flows*, it doesn't grow.

Money flows where consciousness goes! Become more conscious of your relationship to money by using the money mantra: *I am in financial* **flow**, *money comes to me in infinite ways.*

Mt. Everest

A quick and easy way to remind yourself that you do hard stuff on purpose all the time. Climbing Mount Everest is hard, but people climb it. And they do it on purpose, right? Learning another language—for most of you that's really hard but you do it. On purpose. You want to learn to play an instrument. It's challenging, but you do it. On purpose. And then you wonder, "Why is my spiritual life and my spiritual development so hard?" Somehow the difficulty of spiritual development is interpreted as you being a victim of your spiritual path. You are a creator. You are choosing your reactions to your creation. Therefore, take responsibility for your experience and approach it in a new way. Allow yourself to respond with the attitude of, "Yes, this is hard, but I choose it. Just like I choose to climb up a tall mountain or I choose to learn another language, or I choose to learn how to dance ballet. I choose to do hard things all the time. I choose growth and transformation."

On the bus

A cute way of expressing the idea that you are committed to a specific path or idea. We commonly use it to indicate that you are committed to the path of ascension.

Overachieving light worker

A playful description used to illuminate when light workers start thinking, "I have to keep pushing, pushing, pushing to get to that outcome." This is doing rather than being. It is very common to apply the "doing" mentality to the spiritual journey. Part of spiritual transformation is healing this habit.

When you are playing with the overachieving light worker idea, it is all about winning, getting an A+, getting a gold star, being first in line, being on the bus, getting to ascension as fast as you possibly can. In this, there is the risk of losing sight of the fact that "now" is the end result, is the goal, is the desire, is the point of it all. "Now," what you're doing right now, is it.

Peace

Peace is the experience of you being non-disturbable. It is the idea that no matter what's going on you know what your center is. You know the truth of you and you don't resist it. You can have peace even with things you hate about yourself if you don't resist the truth of you being present. Peace is:

"No matter what's going on, I'm still me. No matter who's triggering me, I'm still me."

Personality

The aspect of the incarnate human that has a name, that has preferences, that has a history, that has a future, that has relationships. It's the aspect of you that's currently under development.

The power of the personality is that it wields free will. Therefore, the personality actually is completely in charge of the incarnation by controlling whether or not consciousness is employed, deciding how to react to situations, and deciding whether or not to pursue ascension.

Power

When you live in scarcity—the feeling of lack, fear, guilt, and unconscious low vibration—one of the most popular ways to cope is to exert, or believe you can exert, power over others. The sense that you control another's destiny provides a (false) sense of certainty about one's self.

Control and power do not create safety. Control and power simply require more and more control and power. It's a never-ending cycle.

The only thing to seek power over is power over your habits. The only person you can actually control is yourself; use free-will to choose to change.

Proof

Proof is the repeated demand for certainty, the demand for your eyes to see it in order for you to believe it. Proof is the biggest barrier between you and living an expanded sense of yourself, because the need for proof comes from the small mind. "Prove it to me" is a defiant statement of unconsciousness. Thus it is one of our least-favorite terms because it's so deeply ingrained in the victim mentality. It doesn't have any belief in creatorship or the ability to open to new possibilities without certainty being promised. Your soul's perspective will illuminate many things that can't be proven to the small mind. Will you let the habit of needing proof result in you missing out on these new experiences?

Protect what's mine

This is all about the idea that there's not enough for everyone. It's the notion that, whatever you have, you must make sure no one gets it. You must ensure that you will always have enough. This fallacy is twofold. One, that there's not enough for everyone, and two, that if you have it, it will be enough. It's the idea that if you have enough food set aside, you'll always have food—but eventually, that food gets used, eaten, spoiled, and then there's never enough. It comes from the perspective of lack and the dreaded "h" word—hoarding—which is one of the lowest-vibrational words you have.

Safety

The idea that you can control outcomes. Safety is sought by looking for certainty. Certainty is a fallacy—it can never be achieved. Everything has some degree of uncertainty in it. The survival instinct constantly pushes you to seek safety; the fear-based operating system gives you no way to get there. The ascension journey helps you learn that the only sense of true safety comes from a deep connection to your soul and moving moment to moment through clarity.

Sandpaper/Sandpaper people

A metaphor for the way triggers and fears can be viewed as opportunities for change and growth the way sandpaper shapes a piece of wood: an opportunity to smooth your edges.

Sandpaper people describes relationships that give you an opportunity to grow and transform, typically in an uncomfortable way.

It is never used to indicate victimhood, but rather is a reminder to be conscious that the person or situation is there for your growth.

Serenity

The experience of, "I don't have to seek outside of myself for completeness." A state that has no opposite.

Service mentality

The mistaken idea that you should put another's journey before yours; believing your needs are secondary to others' needs; the idea that "doing good in the world" comes before caring for yourself.

The most powerful way you can be in the world is by loving yourself well and then walking your life from the place of loving yourself well. When you love yourself well, you give the greatest gift you have to give, and that is emanating your uniqueness. Until you love yourself well, you're not really giving a gift. You're simply doing. You're doing and doing and doing in the world. But there's no flavor. There's no taste.

Healthy service is asking, "How can I emanate the highest possible vibration?"

If you choose to offer yourself in service, the first step is to ask your soul for insight, "What is it that best serves me in serving others, in offering myself to others? What serves me first, where will I grow the most?" You want to be in the most conscious frame of mind possible in order to interact at the highest vibrational level possible. Your emanation is your true gift.

Through the act of loving yourself, you give the gift of the truth of you to this world. There is no truth of you until it includes loving yourself. It doesn't exist. "Empty calories" is a way to say it.

We see folks putting themselves out there in the world, saying, "I want everyone to feel better, to feel happier, to have more, to be in a good space." The idea is that taking care of everyone else first is going to be the path to your own bliss, your own peace, your own joy. We have not seen this work well long-term.

People who live to serve others appear energetically drained because their own needs have not been precious to them. They're missing the core amount of attention, of rest, of nourishment, of peace, of quiet, of meditation, of walking, or dancing, whatever it is that feeds them as a person and keeps them whole. Folks in service mentality have been letting pieces of those things go to other people because they think, "Well, if they're happy, I'll be happy, or at least I won't be so distracted by their needs."

The path out of this is to set boundaries. Boundaries don't mean: "I don't love you anymore." Boundaries mean: "I have to love myself first so I have extra love to give. I can't give from this place. I have to give from a whole place." If you keep giving from weakness, eventually you will have nothing left. If you set boundaries, you will rejuvenate yourself.

Unhealthy service mentality can be highly triggered when there are large "disasters." You see something on the news and you think, "Oh my God, those people, they don't have any place to live." You look in your checkbook and you send off whatever you can send off and you think, "I wish I could do more." If you feel that your money, time, or skills are the only way to "serve," then you will often be frustrated. Remember, healthy service is asking, "How can I emanate the highest possible vibration?"

Investing in your energetic and raising your vibration is really the way you meet your desire to help the world. The key here is that you realize that as you raise your vibration and live more consciously, your awareness of others' needs will expand yet your ability to *physically* interact with their needs will not. Use your free will to decide where you want to physically interact with others. How you manage your reaction to the areas where you are aware of the needs of others, yet cannot physically interact with them, is a spiritual challenge best handled by becoming more conscious, which raises your vibration and increases your emanation.

It may be tempting to be so overwhelmed by the many "problems" in the world that you do nothing, including work on yourself. We remind you, emanating your truth into the world is powerfully transformative. That's the greatest gift you can give to yourself and to the world.

Shadow

The aspects of yourself that you don't want anybody else to know about; the things that you are ashamed of and deny, and repress; places where you don't love yourself yet, parts of you that you reject as unacceptable, wrong, bad, or even evil; aspects of your life you feel are socially unacceptable yet still true; honest experiences that you have had that you didn't handle with consciousness; shame: these from your shadow.

We see your shadow aspects as dark holes or gray areas in your energy body that make you look a bit like Swiss cheese.

Our desire is to help you love all parts of yourself, which allows you to live from the soul's perspective as a Homo spiritus being.

Shake shoulders

Demanding attention, insisting that you be listened to, trying to change someone, needing people to agree with you so you will feel safe. The accompanying visual is that you are shaking someone by the shoulders and preaching to them. You may not actually do that, but energetically that's what's going on.

Soul

The infinite, immortal nature of your true self, including the collection of every lifetime you've had on Earth, the time between lifetimes, every lifetime you've had in other incarnational opportunities, and all other experiences.

The soul is a vast reservoir of experience and an eternally curious being.

Animating a human body does not require the entirety of your soul. There is no way you can stuff an entire soul into a human body. But there's a percentage of your soul that has been allocated to be experience-able in this lifetime.

Soulmate

Humans desire safety, and typically believe they need something outside themselves to be safe. That search for something outside of themselves is 'spiritualized' to become "soulmate." The idea is that, "There's another soul out there that is destined to complete me; then I will feel safe." The truth is that all souls reflect the completeness of the creation. No one soul is more able to complete you than any other because that's just not how it works. You are a complete being experiencing the physical life.

That said, because you incarnate in soul groups, there can be souls that you are more familiar with and can feel more connected to simply through familiarity and decisions made in pre-birth planning to share certain experiences. But the quest for a soulmate to complete you is a great, great spiritual fallacy. The quest for a human to partner with or to spend time with in order to facilitate growth is a completely different matter. It can also be a friend, parent, lover, dog, cat, or anything that facilitates spiritual growth. Everything can be used by the incarnate human to facilitate growth, but no one person is specifically sent here to complete you.

So, if soulmate is perceived as someone who is going to complete you, we don't buy into that. But if soulmate is perceived as someone who is going to facilitate your growth, who may or may not stick around for a long time in your life, then that's a more healthy way to use that term. But we advise not using it at all. The implication is that somehow you're not fully you unless this person comes along, and that's lack.

Soul's perspective

The wisdom of your soul incorporated into your experience of being human. It's the insight available to you when you live from the consciousness-based operating system.

From the soul's perspective, there is no judgment, no duality, no fear about life in the physical form. Everything is fascinating.

Your soul knows this is all just a journey in learning. There's no right, there's no wrong, there's no good, there's no bad. It's a journey in learning, exploration, experience. It's not the destination—it's the journey.

Spirituality

Functioning from more than just the survival instinct. Awareness of and openness to experiences outside of those that are "provable" or "repeatable." Knowledge that you are more than just this human form.

Spiritual discipline

When you think, "I don't feel good in this environment," spiritual discipline says, "This is hard, but I'm going to do it." It's challenging, right? You use your spiritual choice and you consciously work with an experience that you wish to change. It's spiritual discipline to align free will with the desire for evolutionary change, and to persevere. Choose and choose again for the growth you desire.

Spiritual growth

Another term for transformation and learning, indicating that your learning is not based on your mind or habits but on consciousness-based transformation.

Static

Unconscious reactions and thoughts; coping mechanisms, masks, lies, baggage, dishonesty, hiding from your authentic expression or the completeness of you; anything that interrupts your ability to stay in the authentic truth of the moment. The mind, the survival instinct, the body, and fear all generate static to keep you small.

Static includes all the reasons you have sold yourself on which you use to avoid presenting the truth of you to the world. It will crop up more intensely as you start to recognize the greatness and the vastness of your true self.

Living consciously is the path to clearing static.

Suffering

Suffering occurs when you experience the world from a victim mentality—not believing you are a creator and instead living in limitation and habit.

You've all suffered, and you have the choice in the suffering to experience it as learning. No matter what is occurring, there's always that choice. Change happens. What is, is. Let's look at it from a new perspective. Do you want to climb out of this new experience with something learned from it, or do you want to wallow in what happened to you, in victimhood?

Survival Instinct

A body-based dynamic that puts the continuation of life at the top of the list of importance. The survival instinct serves you deeply by continuing life even when physical, mental, or emotional experiences lead you to feeling as though you want your life to end.

There had to be a survival instinct put into the system because duality is so different from your experience of being a soul that it would be very tempting to "drop one toe into this water" and then run away. The body's innate survival instinct keeps you in the incarnation long enough to be able to make conscious choices about the experience.

In order to live a conscious life, one must transform one's relationship to the survival instinct. Consciousness asks you to make steps toward change that the survival instinct will be resistant to embrace because to the body, any change feels like potential death and therefore, should be avoided at all costs.

The survival instinct is one of your greatest treasures as well as one of the most challenging places to transform with consciousness because it's so deeply based in the body, and based in unconscious processing. When you are able to consciously modify the way the survival instinct works in the incarnation, you open yourself up to a deep and profound way of re-experiencing how it is to be human. This is one of the major steps in living as Homo spiritus, as an ascended being.

Thinking

The process by which the brain exerts control over the incarnation.

The survival instinct is often the driving force behind thinking.

Thinking is often employed to avoid experiencing change, transformation, or growth. In the spiritual journey, transforming your thought process with consciousness to choose insight from your soul rather than small-mind thinking is one of the major steps to becoming an ascended being.

The brain is the thinking organ. The mind is the thought process. Insight, which comes from your soul, can feel like thinking, however, the content will clarify if you are thinking or receiving insight.

Time

A body-based system by which control is exerted over the incarnation to try to calm the survival instinct into belief that certainty is possible. Time, the passage of time, and the knowledge of when things should be done and how they should be done, helps to make the body feel as though correct, safe, and/or secure action is taking place.

When you recognize that you are living from insight from your soul, from one "aha" to the next, you will no longer need "time" to make you feel safe. You will live in one expanded moment. How that one expanded moment will interact with the turning of the planet and the change of the seasons is a glorious exploration that we anticipate will keep you entertained and enchanted for what you would refer to, in time, as many years.

When you remove time as a controlling factor, what you perceive as time—or changes over time—becomes a tapestry you weave rather than the master with the whip telling you how to live.

Tools

Techniques used to interrupt the unconscious running of habit by using consciousness to shift out of a fear-based operating system into the consciousness-based operating system. See the table of contents for a list of tools included in this book.

Transformation

A term describing change, especially change along the ascension process.

Triggers

Triggers are stimuli that the personality experiences which bring up opportunities to explore unhealed parts of the personality self.

Triggers are handholds

Triggers are the handholds on the climbing wall of ascension. Triggers are not to be avoided or run from. Triggers are to be embraced as opportunities for progress. Now, we understand that triggers have made you spin and suffer, and it's very hard to see them as an opportunity, but's still true; triggers are handholds on the climbing wall of ascension.

When you contemplate climbing up one of those climbing walls—you all have seen these walls with the different places to put your hands and your feet—you see the next handhold and you think, "OK, I think I can make it to that one, I think I can reach that one," you're grateful that handhold is there because that handhold takes you up to where you want to go. This is how we would like you to look at fear, guilt, lack, anger, and other low-vibrational states; look at them as though they are a handhold on a climbing wall. Because that's what they are; they're the way you get where you want to go.

When a fear comes up, grab it with both hands and say, "Thank you for being here. I need this handhold. I want you here so I can grow. I put healing above all else. I want ascension. I'm going to the top of whatever this thing is. I'm going to make you a handhold." Seize them with the same intensity, gratitude, and upliftment that that next handhold would give you if you were climbing a mountain.

When you get to the top, all the transformed triggers are the foundation under your feet. You see? You climb and you climb and you transform and you transform and then you get to the top and what do you do? You get to look out at the view. You get to see a new perspective. All of a sudden there's a vista. But that vista is only possible because of the experiences that lifted you up that wall. All those handholds, all those triggers, all those places where you slipped a little bit, they all helped you become the new you.

Unconscious

Acting from the fear-based operating system without the intervention of consciousness; running habit.

Understanding is overrated

You've been taught that "understanding" is a worthy goal. You use your amazing brain to "wrap your mind around" something until you understand it. We say "understanding is overrated" to remind you that understanding something with your mind isn't the only way you can interact with it. There is a vast amount of insight from your soul that you can access on any subject. Reminding yourself that "understanding is overrated" will help you break the habit of limited thinking and remember to open to your soul's perspective.

If thinking could have solved it, it would have solved it long ago because you sure have thought about it enough! Open to insight and add your soul's perspective to the mix.

Unfolding

While you're in the process of transformation, it unfolds like a rose opening; you never quite know what the next step is going to be, just like you never know what the next petal of the rose is going to look like until it opens and unfolds. On your unique journey, you experience something that's never been experienced before—the unfolding truth of you which is gradually revealed as you walk the path of consciousness.

Vibration

Low vibration: A state of being that comes from living from the fear-based operating system, not looking for conscious understanding or experience of the dynamics being presented to you. Living habitually rather than opening to new experience.

It is not a judgmental term, rather it is descriptive of the fact that your body is actually vibrating at a different rate than it would if you infused consciousness into your life.

Your soul vibrates at a very high rate. It is difficult to connect to your soul's energy when living a low-vibrational life.

High-vibration: A description of actions, thoughts, ideas, and relationships which are based on consciousness and conscious choices. It is not a judgmental term, rather it is descriptive of the fact that your body is actually vibrating at a different rate than it did before you infused consciousness into your life.

Your soul vibrates at a very high rate. Raising your vibration by living consciously is a very important step in living from your soul's perspective and walking the path of ascension.

Victim/Victimhood

The mistaken perspective that things happen to you that you are at the whim of any other creature, being, person, or eventuality that you experience while on Earth. Running the fear-based operating system. It is a perspective that is very easy to assume because you incarnate with amnesia, making it difficult for you to remember your infinite nature, or the fact that you planned to be here and have the experiences you are having.

When events trigger you or you have experiences that you deem negative, your reaction is, "Why did this happen to me?" which is a victim's perspective. With a conscious journey and a conscious life, you're able to start seeing the world as the creator that you are, and start asking, "Why is this happening *for* me?" and realizing that "Everything teaches me something."

Woman by the campfire

We use this phrase as a quick way to describe the following energetic: "If my man doesn't come home to me, I die." This energetic is part of your DNA, it's in your cells, it's part of your culture, but primarily it comes from alternate expressions where this was much more of a reality: If your man took the meat from his hunt to *her* fire instead of yours, you and your kids could literally starve to death.

It's also a shortcut way of saying, "I am hard-wired to believe something that I haven't consciously explored."

As you shift out of Homo sapiens into Homo spiritus one of the major differences between the two states is understanding the influence you have, using consciousness, over the biological reactions as presented by the body doing its normal job. Just as the body keeps breathing and the heart keeps beating and the blood keeps moving and all that stuff keeps happening, habits keep getting thrown up in front of you. Not just the habit of fear, but the idea of lack, the idea of safety, the idea of security, abundance all these issues that you've habituated that are part of your biology.

Biological reactions to stimulus that previously haven't been run through consciousness are now coming under your influence. As you move out of the Homo sapiens mindset into the Homo spiritus experience it becomes your responsibility to consciously monitor the biological reactions to stimulus. You're responsible for the emanations you create as you react.

This includes pain, emotional stimulus, memory stimulus, and fear stimulus. All of these things that you previously felt were hardwired in you can become the purview of your conscious exploration.

Your internal world creates your external journey

Your internal world is the creation point for the external expression of your life. Not the other way around. Your internal process is projected on the movie screen of your external life where it all plays out. This allows you to learn and grow from the experience of observing your internal life projected (externalized).

Your internal world is a series of choices that you've made, even if the choice was to default to a habitual pattern, to default to a culturally driven pattern, to default to the childhood pattern. Those are still choices.

Remember, it can't happen in your external world unless it's true in your internal world. When experiences arise, ask, "What are you showing me about me? What are you telling me about me?" Let the experiences inform you rather than staying with the surface reaction of, "They're just triggering me or challenging me or frustrating me or driving me bananas." Ask instead, "What are you showing me about me?"

You can't dictate how people react to you, necessarily, but you can certainly influence the outcome by loving yourself well and sending that into the world instead of doubt and anguish and anxiety and feeling stepped on and being a victim and all that. If you walk into a room knowing you love yourself and emanating your truth, you're going to have a different experience than if you walk into a room feeling like a victim and a doormat. You will be known and reacted to by the way you love yourself.

Your awareness of your internal world becomes so rich and well-developed, so well-known and mapped by you, that your emanation of the truth of your internal world starts to resemble a fountain that bubbles up and spills over without stopping. It's not something you have to think about or work yourself through or get going. It bubbles up in you and it spills over, just like a fountain does, the fullness of your internal world emanating out into the world. This doesn't involve you acting in the world as much as it involves you experiencing the world from your truth. The truth of you being real.

About the author

Photo credit: nancikerby.com

Veronica Torres: is based in Sonoma, CA. She has channeled Eloheim since 2002, both in public and private sessions. Her public channeling sessions are offered five times a month. These sessions are broadcast live on the Internet and archived for on-demand viewing.

Veronica's career history is interesting and varied, with work including: talk radio host, Rock and Roll memorabilia store owner, Network Director of a Holistic Practitioner's Group, Producer of Well Being Expos, and jewelry designer!

What is channeling?

Channeling is a process where I set my personality aside to allow Eloheim and The Council to use my physical form to convey their teachings.

PLEASE NOTE: This is not possession. It only occurs when I give explicit permission. I can stop it at ANY time.

When I am channeling I feel as though I am standing or sitting behind and to the left of my actual body. I am aware of what is being said as the session unfolds, although I don't always remember everything that is discussed.

Eloheim and The Council specialize in reading the energy of a question, situation, or person. They often experience visual representations of the energy they sense. When this occurs, I see it as a "movie" in my head not unlike what happens when I am dreaming.

I have created a YouTube video with more details about the process. You can watch it by following this link http://youtube.com/EJ2rVvBsB1c.

Who are Eloheim and The Council?

On February 11, 1997, I had a reading by a very skilled psychic and channel. During that reading he said that I would become a channel myself. Although I valued much of what he shared, my reaction to that statement was, YEAH, RIGHT!

I was quite familiar with channeling. I found it incredibly valuable. I just didn't see myself doing it!

That all changed when I came to Sonoma. I was invited to a friend's home to do a Lakshmi puja. The chanting left me in a very altered state. When we finished, we sat in a circle on the floor. I told one of the participants I had a message for her and then shared information she found very helpful. At the end of the sharing I said, "We are the Eloheim and we are pleased to have been with you today."

Now, even though I knew what had happened, I was overwhelmed by it and started to cry. It didn't feel bad or wrong, just very intense. It made me feel very conspicuous. I immediately told myself, "That's never going to happen again."

It was some time before it did. Over time, I got more comfortable with the idea of being a channel but I had no idea how to do it! I tried to work with Eloheim on my own once or twice. I even recorded a very useful message about habitual response on November 26, 2000, yet it just wasn't coming together. Almost two years passed without much forward movement.

Finally, a friend and I figured it out. What was needed was a second person to ask the questions and help me with the logistics of the whole thing.

In the very beginning while channeling, I had to raise my right hand in order to receive the energies (boy, am I glad that I don't have to do that any longer). I would get very thirsty, but I wasn't able to hold a glass (I still have a bunch of straws in a drawer from those days). I had a TON of insecurity about "Am I making this up?" and "Is this real?" and "Am I doing it right?" I needed a lot of reassurance just to stick with it. I would get very sleepy afterward and sometimes needed help just getting around. I had to eat a lot of protein to keep my energy level up.

Details, details, details. All of which felt completely unmanageable to me alone, but became possible once I had help.

After about one month, Eloheim told us that this wasn't just for the two of us and to get a group together. That was September 2002, when we began our weekly Eloheim sessions. We still hold meetings every Wednesday night and one Sunday per month. You can join us live or tune into our webcasts. For more information, please visit: eloheim.com/web-casts.

I had never heard the term Eloheim until they introduced themselves that way. Someone then told me it was one of the names of God. I looked it up on the Internet and found that to be true. It is important to note that although it is common to see the spelling Elohim, I was guided to use the spelling Eloheim.

Eloheim has made it clear that just as not everyone named John is the same, to not assume that all entities using the name Eloheim or Elohim are the same. The material they present with me is internally consistent and can be taken as a whole.

Eloheim is a group entity that presents with one voice. That one voice feels like a male energy. We refer to the Eloheim as "he" or "they."

They refer to themselves as "we."

Starting on June 10, 2009, I began channeling the rest of The Council. Here are the dates of their first appearances:

The Visionaries - 06/10/2009

The Guardians - 12/02/2009

The Girls - 01/06/2010

The Matriarch - 02/03/2010

The Warrior - 03/17/2010

Fred - 06/30/2010

For more information about Eloheim and The Council, please visit:

eloheim.com/who-is-eloheim

Contact

Website: Eloheim.com

Facebook: Facebook.com/eloheim

Twitter: twitter.com/channelers

YouTube: youtube.com/eloheimchannel

Join our live channeling sessions in person or online:

eloheim.com/web-casts

Visit our meeting archives for video and audio recordings of past gatherings:

eloheim.com/eloheim-recordings

Join our mailing list:

tinyurl.com/eloheimlist

Preview of other books

Eloheim and The Council books are available online through major eBook retailers and by visiting http://www.eloheim.com/dlg/cart/index.php.

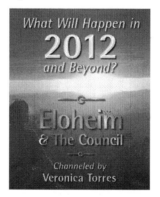

What Will Happen in 2012 and Beyond?

The question, "What will happen in 2012?" is being asked by a great many people. The Mayan calendar ends on December 21, 2012 which has given rise to a considerable amount of speculation about what might happen, including predictions that the world will either end or that we will experience some sort of catastrophic event.

With so much fear and uncertainty surrounding "What will happen in 2012?", we decided to ask Eloheim for their perspective.

IN THIS **57** PAGE BOOK, ELOHEIM ANSWERS THE FOLLOWING QUESTIONS:

What did the Mayans know about 2012 and why does their calendar end in December of 2012?; Why did the Hopi point to 2012 and say any chance at salvation is now useless as we have gone too far?; Why is there so much fear about 2012?

Isn't it pretty likely there will be one or more disasters in the future?; Is it true that the Earth's population will be reduced to 500 million?; Will Jesus reappear in 2012?; Will aliens rescue the surviving population like a modern Noah's ark?; Are aliens already here?; Is the Earth going to be like a cell dividing in two—people who ascend going with the new Earth and the others staying behind thinking the rest are dead or gone?

Will there be a nuclear war or will the Earth be hit by an asteroid causing an ice age?; Are pole shifts occurring that may cause chaos in 2012? How about solar flares causing Earth disturbances?; Is it true that a civilization will emerge from middle Earth in 2012?; Is overpopulation going to cause a disaster in 2012?

We learn by crisis. Does it appear that we're getting it or do we need bigger and bigger crises to move ahead?; Regarding 2012, are there any safe areas?; If it's true that everyone is going to ascend anyway, what's the point in all the work that we're doing?; How can I deal with my fear and anxiety regarding 2012? Is there anything I should do to prepare for it?; What will happen after 2012?

The book also contains four of Eloheim's tools for spiritual growth: Point fingers; What's in your lap?; What is true now?; and You to you. Additionally, there are 62 definitions of terms and concepts including: ascension, creating your reality, consciousness-based operating system, energetics, ensoulment, free will, Homo spiritus, shadow, soul's perspective, transformation, vibration, and your internal world creates your external experience.

Use the energy of 2012 to facilitate your personal growth!—Eloheim

The Choice for Consciousness: Tools for Conscious Living, Vol. 1

Why would you want to make the choice for consciousness? What are tools for conscious living?

Two very important questions.

Here are four more: Are you living in peace? Are you living in joy? Are you living in serenity? Are you living in bliss?

And, the most important question: Are you ready to take bold steps in that direction?

Moving out of a fear-based operating system into a consciousness-based operating system allows you to experience being human in a brand-new way. A way that isn't driven by habit, repetitive thinking, reliving the past, speculating about the future, or being paralyzed by the fear of change.

Consciousness is a way of living that focuses on an authentic experience of the moment, awareness of your truth, and the full comprehension that by choosing your reaction to every one of your experiences, you are creating your reality.

This book contains simple but powerful tools that will help you make the shift from the fear-based operating system (survival) to the consciousness-based operating system (fascination).

These tools can be used throughout your spiritual journey. They require no props, no rituals, no religious beliefs, and can be easily incorporated into your day-to-day activities. In addition, they build on one another and can be used in powerful combinations that will rapidly transform your experience.

The first section introduces 22 tools. The second section defines and clarifies nearly 100 terms and concepts. You can read this volume in any order. It is not a narrative, but a reference book you will likely turn to time and time again.

***

The Homo Spiritus Sessions, Collection One

COLLECTION ONE includes transcripts of EIGHT Eloheim and The Council channeling sessions held between July 7, 2010 and August 25, 2010.

It's not WHY is this happening? It's WOW this is happening! Experiences are here to facilitate growth, expansion, and transformation. Nothing happens TO you; it all happens FOR you. You create your reality by choosing your reactions to your experiences.

The spiritual journey is a natural process of expansion (growth) and contraction (contemplation). Through this process, you discover the truth of you and learn to emanate that truth into the world. Empower yourself by discerning the difference between vulnerability and weakness. Evolve your relationship to the survival instinct; don't let fear and habits tell you who you are!

The truth of you is emanated into the world through your choices about how you react to your creations. If issues come up again, it doesn't mean you're broken, it means you're going deeper.

Feelings are not emotions! Feelings are a deep and powerful pathway to ascension based on what is actually occurring in this moment. Emotions are habitually, biologically, and/or culturally based. Be vulnerable. Tell the truth. Be honest about your feelings. Be willing to admit when you want to learn something. Open to the fact that you don't know everything.

When you're tempted to be in the past or the future, we invite you to say: "Am I courageous enough to be with me now? Am I courageous enough to attend to my concerns about me, fascination with me, my insight about me? Am I courageous enough to do that?"

Where do you feel unlovable? The answer is the doorway to the next level of your spiritual growth. The true nature of your infinite, and immortal self resides just a breath away in any moment, and it exists for you to access at any time.

The Homo Spiritus Sessions series offers channeled messages from Eloheim and The Council.

The Council is comprised of seven different groups: The Guardians, The Girls, The Visionaries, The Matriarch, The Eloheim, The Warrior, and Fred. During a channeling session, each of The Council members take turns sharing their teachings. Each Council member has a distinct personality, style of delivery, and focus.

The Council is best known for their multitude of practical tools, which support our journey out of the fear-based operating system into the consciousness-based operating system.

COLLECTION ONE INCLUDES **29** TOOLS:

Big toe, left elbow; Choose and choose again; Color with all the crayons; Don't be mean to yourself; Equal signs; Feelings are not emotions; Feet under shoulders; Go to the bathroom; How ridiculous does it have to get?; Mad Scientist; Money mantra; Neutral observation; "No" is a complete sentence; Point fingers; Preferences/Judgments; Re-queue; Script holding; Short, factual statements; Velcro; Vulnerability vs. weakness; What is in your lap?; What is IS; What is true now?; Where am I lying to myself?; Who answers the door?; Why, why, why?; Wow!, not why?; You can't have change without change; You to you (compare).

ADDITIONALLY, **COLLECTION ONE** INCLUDES **126** DEFINITIONS OF TERMS AND CONCEPTS.

Each of the *Homo Spiritus Sessions* books can stand alone, but taken together will allow the reader to follow along with the progression of the teachings including the introduction, in-depth explanation, and evolution of The Council's tools.

***

Eloheim and The Council books are available online through major eBook retailers and by visiting eloheim.com/dlg/cart/index.php.